A.W.E.S.O.M.E.

7 Keys to Unlock the Speaker Within

JESS PONCE III
AND EMILY LIU

2219 West Olive Avenue, #148
Burbank, California 91506

Library of Congress Control Number: 2020922438
Paperback ISBN: 978-0998562322
Digital ISBN: 978-0998562339

Dedication

To my younger self.
The fear that once held you back
is now the fuel that drives me forward.
Thank you for not giving up.

Contents

Preface 1

    Behind the Mask 1

    Finding Value 3

Introduction 7

    What is public speaking? 7

    Be the Message 8

    An Awesome Beginning 9

    An Entertainment Angle 11

    How to Use this Book 12

SECTION I: The Foundation 15

    Chapter 1: The A.W.E.S.O.M.E Idea 17

    Chapter 2: The Guiding Principles 25

SECTION II: Surrender 37

    Chapter 3: What's Fear Got to Do with It 39

    Chapter 4: The Audience is Listening 55

    Chapter 5: The Powerful Dialogue Within 69

SECTION III: The A.W.E.S.O.M.E You 91

    Chapter 6: Aligned 93

    Chapter 7: Wired 109

Chapter 8: Empathetic. 125

Chapter 9: Simple 143

Chapter 10: Open 159

Chapter 11: Magical 175

Chapter 12: Engaging 191

SECTION IV: A.W.E.S.O.M.E Talk 209

Chapter 13: Tell Your Story. 211

Chapter 14: S.P.E.A.K. 225

Chapter 15: More than "15 Minutes of Fame" 241

SECTION V: Be the Message 255

Chapter 16: Self-Declarations, Perceptions, and

Assessments 257

Chapter 17: Step Up, Speak Out, Be Heard. 275

SECTION VI: Reference Guide and Key Terms 281

A.W.E.S.O.M.E. Flow Chart 283

15 Key Concepts for Being A.W.E.S.O.M.E. 285

10 Mantras for Being an A.W.E.S.O.M.E. Speaker . 291

About the Authors. 293

About the Entertainment Professionals Featured

in A.W.E.S.O.M.E. 297

Acknowledgments 303

Testimonials 305

Preface

Behind the Mask

What had I done? Immediately and instinctively, I knew it wasn't right. It wasn't me.

I was seventeen years old, a junior in high school, and running for student body treasurer. In front of the entire school, out on the football field, it was time for us to give our speeches. I had originally prepared a thoughtful and sincere discourse about why I should be elected, but the night before, I changed my mind. Instead, I went for a gimmick.

Shortly after introducing myself, I put on a mask... literally and figuratively. I thought this prop would somehow illustrate how I believed my opponent came across: contrived and insincere. As I put on this homemade mask—a paper plate with holes for eyes and a mouth—I realized that I was demonstrating the exact traits I was criticizing. As I stood there, it struck me that I was the one who was inauthentic.

I'd made a big mistake.

When I took off the mask, an awkward silence filled the arena. The audience shifted in their seats, chuckled uncomfortably, and followed with a polite and subdued applause.

As I quickly took my seat, my opponent stepped up to the podium, smiled and said playfully, "Um, I don't quite know what to say." The audience roared with laughter.

They were laughing at me.

I don't remember what my opponent said after his initial greeting, but they were words and actions that definitely engaged the audience.

Needless to say, I didn't win that election. In fact, it was my fourth and final attempt at running for a student office. It was my last effort to be popular—something I realized years later I wanted much more than I could admit then.

I wanted to be seen, heard, and admired. I wanted to be liked for being Jess. After all, who doesn't want this in high school – or even in adulthood?

Putting on a mask, focusing on something outside of you, and trying too hard aren't the answers. As I so painfully learned, those tactics don't work. The impression you make when you try too hard usually does not reflect the person you really are.

Before I put on the mask, I had a gut feeling that it was the wrong thing to do, but fear overtook me. I ignored my

Preface

better judgment, knowing this action wouldn't serve me. Even now, I am embarrassed by what others saw in me that day, but I am more ashamed by what I witnessed in myself. I didn't trust that I was enough.

I had no idea that inside was a shining, unique me waiting to be seen. I knew I had a gift to lead and inspire, but I had no tools to harness it and use it.

In my insecurity, I decided to focus on my opponent's limitations instead of showcasing my own strengths. In the end, I pulled a stunt and it fell flat.

It was a harsh lesson to learn.

In that moment of attacking my opponent, I surrendered my own power. An inner strength was always there. I just didn't know it or have the confidence to use it.

Today I am more aware of that power. I see it. I feel it. I listen to that internal voice.

The benefit of hindsight. Since that experience on the podium, I learned to trust my gut, acknowledge my fears, and show up as the best me possible in the moment.

Finding Value

The quest to find real value in myself and in others became my lifelong passion.

A.W.E.S.O.M.E.

For years I wanted to *be somebody*. To be acknowledged and appreciated. Winning that election would have meant my peers accepted me. It would have meant they liked me. I was looking to them for validation.

That afternoon on the football field, I learned not to try so hard.

As the son of a salesman and a purchasing agent, my first exposure to the professional world was to look at things through a lens of *value.* How do you get others to see why a product is valuable?

You have to know your audience, understand how this product can satisfy their needs, and promote it so they buy it.

Communicating value with intention and clarity is my mission in this world. As a media and communication coach in the entertainment industry, I help clients craft messages so they can be strategic and purposeful in their communication. Specifically, I coach them to communicate their true value: **who they are** as individuals and experts and **how to identify their irresistible offer**. When they identify this irresistible offer, they can present their best selves.

Sometimes you will find yourselves with a mic in hand— sometimes by choice and other times by circumstance. In those moments you must face whatever fear of public speaking you might have. If you're organized, know your

Preface

irresistible offer, and believe what you have to offer is valuable, you will shine. But it does take preparation. And intention.

That's where I step in.

As I have with celebrities, experts, and other well-known personalities, I will guide you to discover your own formula for bringing out your best in public speaking, regardless of the situation. I will help you to communicate clearly who you are and to create your own personal blueprint for delivering compelling messages and irresistible offers that get the results you deserve.

Introduction

What is public speaking?

Every time you communicate an idea or experience to others, you engage in public speaking. Your beliefs are shaped into words, heard by others and, therefore, are no longer just yours. They are a gift.

And we need these gifts. There is no value in playing small because our big world is shaped by beautiful convictions like the ones you hold close. Don't hold back.

After all, we are all presenters. We are all storytellers. We are all performers sharing our unique points of view.

This happens in many different ways: job interviews, political speeches, press events, keynotes, and toasts at social events. It also happens in ways we may not consider, like social media or conversations you have with a group of people. While the medium and context may change, the fact is, you are expressing yourself in a public environment.

You engage in some form of public speaking almost daily. You reveal yourself whether or not you are aware of it. And when you are prepared, others experience you the way you want them to witness you.

A.W.E.S.O.M.E.

Be the Message

Many of us focus only on the physical aspects of public speaking—tone of voice, pacing, body position, and eye contact. While these factors certainly influence one's impact, focusing only on "how" to speak limits a person's unique potential.

What you say only has value if it's grounded in who you are. What shows up on the outside must align with what is on the inside. Cultivating your own speaking style emerges when your words, thoughts, and emotions work together in unison as a vehicle of expression.

Look at your everyday interactions. Are you outspoken or subtle? Are you dramatic or analytical? Are you deep or light in your approach? Examining your innate nature aligns with the way you best communicate with others. This is what makes *you*—not everyone else—a good speaker.

You already have the power within to be an effective speaker. Unknowingly, you've been harnessing it for years. The challenge is to recognize and use it.

It is a call to be A.W.E.S.O.M.E.—an inward journey to pull out and put to use your own best speaking potential. There are seven keys to unlocking the speaker within. You become the message. You are:

Introduction

Aligned
Wired
Empathetic
Simple
Open
Magical
Engaging

These keys will serve you as a speaker in every platform.

An Awesome Beginning

For years, separately and together, my business colleague and friend, Emily Liu, and I have helped countless clients deliver powerful messages to their audiences.

A constant innovator, Emily has been revolutionizing the personal and professional development arena in Asia for more than two decades. She's created interactive experiential learning programs, written several books, and brought world-class thought leaders to her organization.

I've been lucky enough to be one of those thought leaders.

In our work together, we have developed communication workshops and programs to help people tap into their innate star quality. Focusing on one's "being" is the foundation of our work.

A.W.E.S.O.M.E.

One of the things we both witnessed firsthand is how individuals are not adequately empowered to overcome their insecurities about public speaking. People are scared to be vulnerable, lack the conviction to take a stand, and can't handle criticism of any kind.

We needed to do something about it.

One night, I was briefing Emily for an upcoming workshop via videoconference from my home office in California while she was in Hong Kong. After we finished, she looked into the camera and said:

> Are you ready? I have an idea... Our trainings are based on "Be-Do-Have." We help people find their essence – their intrinsic nature. Essence is a combination of a person's innate strengths and his vulnerabilities. Essence is vital to developing character, from how we treat others to how we deal with hardships, to how we create opportunity. Essence frees the authentic self and sets the foundation for professional success. Once we understand the power of our essence, then we can better connect with others.

> After more than twenty years of helping people harness their essence, it is time to take the next step. I want to design a platform for others to share their learning— to express how understanding their essence has impacted their personal and professional lives. Specifically, I want to create a one-day public speaking

Introduction

showcase where people we've worked with can inspire others with their own stories of struggle and success.

In the end, Emily's idea—her vision—evolved into a spectacular public speaking tournament: "AWESOME TALK: I speak, therefore I am." Think *TEDx* meets the TV show, *The Voice*.

The process started with thirty contestants who were chosen from video submissions. We mentored them along the way, assisting them to shine and stand out on the stage. We recalibrated the content of their story, designed doable cues, and increased their interactions with the audience. Eight of them made the final cut to give speeches on the stage.

That experience was a turning point in our vision. We'd already had success with the personal transformations of our individual coaching clients based on the workshops we co-created, as well as our first book, *Everyday Celebrity*.

All of this work, combined with the experience of producing the speaking tournament, sparked the creation of this book, *A.W.E.S.O.M.E.*

An Entertainment Angle

TED coaches who write books on public speaking share wonderful points of view based on their firsthand experiences with professional speakers. Their advice helps all readers, regardless of occupation. While not every reader wants to be a professional speaker, the lessons can be applied to any working or personal life.

In this book, I share my firsthand experiences from an entertainment industry perspective as a media and communication coach. While you may not want to be a celebrity, you can speak with the confidence and charisma of one.

I also provide a collection of viewpoints from other professionals in the entertainment business. They are agents, producers, publicists, acting coaches, speakers, media personalities, and more.

These professionals help actors, performers, and well-known personalities own the spotlight. In many ways, they are experts who help celebrities see their own strength and power. Some have called them "kingmakers."

Now, imagine having a team of people—kingmakers—helping *you* develop your *own* personal power. Together we will equip you with techniques and ideas on how to better express yourself through public speaking and create a lasting impression.

How to Use this Book

There is a straightforward formula for each chapter.

1. *Topic*: a concept or idea that builds from chapter to chapter

2. *Story:* taken from clients and/or entertainment industry interviews

3. *Lesson Learned:* what you the reader can get from the story

4. *Summary:* key learning highlights

5. *Exercise:* an activity that you can do on your own

6. *Call to Action:* a take-away to integrate into your speaking today; sometimes expressed as a mantra

My goal is to help you be more successful when you are called to speak in front of others—whether that is at work, in the community, or on the stage. We aim to do this by empowering you to:

- Be in the moment and adapt your message in an impromptu, yet purposeful fashion

- Overcome criticism and turn it into a valuable asset

- Present, speak, and pitch yourself and your business/product/brand like a pro

- Learn how to align your words, heart, and intuition for improved impact

- Engage your audience like a world-class motivator

It's your moment to capture the spotlight. Be heard when it counts… and learn how to shine when you need it most!

SECTION I:

The Foundation

CHAPTER 1
The A.W.E.S.O.M.E. Idea

It starts with an idea.
It becomes real when you speak it.

What is A.W.E.S.O.M.E.?

To be a truly successful speaker, one must use more than words. Powerful speakers—whether they are giving a speech, business pitch, or a toast at a wedding—know how to *be the message*. They understand how to be A.W.E.S.O.M.E.

Being A.W.E.S.O.M.E. is a call to express your best self. It is an inward pilgrimage to unearth the communication skills that inherently exist within you but may have remained dormant. It challenges you to explore and implement seven ways your mind, body, and intuition can work together so you are a more effective and compelling public speaker.

It is a call to be: **A**ligned. **W**ired. **E**mpathetic. **S**imple. **O**pen. **M**agical. **E**ngaging.

Here is a breakdown of what being A.W.E.S.O.M.E. means:

- *Aligned*: Your mind, body, and intuition work in unison as a vehicle of expression.

- *Wired*: You are connected to your surroundings, medium of expression, and audience.

- *Empathetic*: Your focus is on your audience and what they need, want, or feel.

A.W.E.S.O.M.E.

- *Simple:* You are straightforward. Being organic is core. You know that less is more.

- *Open:* You embrace the unexpected. You are connected to your environment and seamlessly integrate unforeseen obstacles with ease and creativity.

- *Magical:* Your intuition is unleashed and your powerful presence is revealed.

- *Engaging:* You masterfully know how to use mediums at your disposal, especially yourself, the ultimate medium.

When speakers embody all these qualities, they are purveyors of an authentic message that is unleashed through their entire body and being.

In the tradition of Emily's "Be-Do-Have" approach, being A.W.E.S.O.M.E. ignites that yearning within to show up, be seen, and be heard. To be seen by others, you must first see yourself clearly. To be heard, you must know with certainty that your voice is valuable.

When you embrace your A.W.E.S.O.M.E. self, you communicate with purpose and the 3 Cs: Clarity, Confidence, and Charisma.

Everyday Celebrity: The Shining Unique You Unleashed

In our first book, *The Shining Unique You* (title in Mandarin)

The A.W.E.S.O.M.E. Idea

and *Everyday Celebrity* (title in English), the 3 Cs—Clarity, Confidence, and Charisma—were introduced. These are the building blocks for your personal *Celebrity Essence* — how you purposefully choose to communicate who you are to others. When you step on stage, whether it is literally or metaphorically, you communicate the best of who you are and what you have to offer.

Celebrities are purposeful in how they show up. They pay special attention to their words, their actions, and their appearance. We can do the same. We just have to show up as our best selves.

Whether at work bussing tables, serving behind the counter at a coffee shop, or guiding tourists on vacation, each of us has a special magnetism that we can harness if we choose to. This is your own *Celebrity Essence*. This quality is the ability to shine when the metaphorical spotlight is on you. It begins when you acknowledge your star quality within.

Celebrity Essence:

- is your personal *star quality*
- proves with certainty that you are a gift to the world
- showcases your personal strengths and attributes
- creates sincere conviction to be purposeful and strategic with your public identity

A.W.E.S.O.M.E.

As a Hollywood media coach, I help celebrities and creative entertainment executives to sparkle with that special something that is innate, but sometimes hard to describe. Emily and I, however, take this to another level. We help people find their *Celebrity Essence*, that "star quality," whether the client is an executive, entrepreneur, influencer, or speaker.

In the entertainment industry, this sort of star quality is also known as the "it" factor—but it's not limited to celebrities.

My friend, Tim Curtis, is a talent agent and partner at WME Entertainment, the largest talent agency in the world. He represents celebrities for endorsements and feature animation, and describes that "it" factor this way:

> It's an intangible quality; it's an aura or a glow that some people have. You can see someone in a line of people and think, "That person has a certain spark." Whether that individual does anything with that spark or not is really up to him or her. Is that person actually talented? Who knows? There's just that extra gift—a little bit more of an edge that person has over somebody who might be equally as—or more—talented. There is a special charisma that glows from within.

Tim explains it in more detail...

You can have that glow and be successful in anything.

It's an energy that will draw people to you, and ultimately give you a boost in whatever profession you're in. You can be an accountant and have that glow, and you're probably going to be a more successful accountant than the person sitting in the cubicle next to you.

How do you harness this special quality and unleash your *Celebrity Essence*?

It starts with a choice. You must be purposeful in how you show up and communicate *who you are* and *what you have to offer*. Be bold, speak up, and show people, like your boss or clients, exactly how irresistible you are. Do not wait, as some do in Hollywood, to be "discovered."

Tim says it's not only about knowing your "it" factor, but also knowing how to showcase it when needed:

> You become a little more self-aware. You work a little harder, push yourself a little bit more, and engage with people in different ways. Let them see more of the inner you versus waiting for them to pick you out from the crowd. You have to step forward and say, "I deserve to be picked."

Connecting Your Celebrity Essence with A.W.E.S.O.M.E.

Be authentic in your approach. Be clear on how you want to be seen. Know and accept your *Celebrity Essence.*

A.W.E.S.O.M.E.

Foster your inner confidence. When you can reach people hungry to hear your message and eager to embrace the real you, a deeper sense of fulfillment can follow.

CHAPTER 2

The Guiding Principles

You are creative, knowledgeable, and intuitive.
Playing small doesn't serve you or others.

Are you ready to shine?

First, accept that you are already a star. You don't need to take center stage on a Broadway play or star in a Hollywood blockbuster movie in order to shine. There is a unique shining you waiting to illuminate. Second, foster your *Celebrity Essence* and learn how to express it when needed most.

To ground you in achieving this, I challenge you to accept and practice the following three guiding principles. These master assessments are overarching beliefs about who you are and your ability to be A.W.E.S.O.M.E. They establish that you are creative, skillful, and instinctual.

Guiding Principle #1: You Are Creative

You are creating all the time. Every day you have creative conversations. They are part of your life and you may not even be aware of it. Simple brainstorming with your spouse or friends about what to have for dinner is designing future action.

You and your partner may make a mutual decision by compromise, or one of you may grant the other authority to pick the dinner outcome. The decision may be based on convenience, taste, location, diet, or a myriad of reasons. Regardless of how the decision is made, you have a dialogue that produces an action and a reality that did not exist before.

A.W.E.S.O.M.E.

It is magic.

This magic, or creation, happens the moment you put your thoughts and ideas into words. When you commit your thinking out loud into the world, you are giving birth to something you no longer hold onto alone. It is communal. It is a gift.

Committing your thoughts to words can be scary. It is this scary emotion that prevents you from speaking and being the creative manifestation you were meant to be.

When you let commitment flow through you, you are creative. The simple conversation about what to eat for dinner is just one small example. Can you think of something more significant, such as a wedding proposal? Or job interview? In both of these situations, you have the ability to create the future.

The words we share with others have an immense creative power because we never know what is going to happen as a result. Here's an example.

The Programming Executive and the Writer

My friend, programming executive Loren Ruch, had one such powerful conversation that created a new future for a mutual friend of ours:

The Guiding Principles

Cindy was stuck in what she felt was a dead-end television production job. She was just not feeling at all like she was living up to her potential and dreams. She always considered herself a writer but didn't know how to break the mold. I believed in her, told her so, and encouraged her to take action. "I'm going to give you an opportunity to write one of our shows." It was a little scary from this side, but I really did believe in her.

We gave her [the opportunity to write for] *Dream Home*, which is a big franchise [for HGTV]. She had never done it before, and she knocked it out of the park. At that moment she realized, "I don't just think I'm a writer; I am a writer."

She quit the job she had and writes full time. That's all she does now. She writes and script-doctors TV shows for a living. She just needed someone to believe in her.

Loren's words impacted Cindy's life in an extraordinary way, by simply telling her that he believed in her.

What do you believe in? What do you create with your own words, either internally or out loud to the world? Your words, once committed out loud, take form in a remarkable way. They have the power to impact one person or thousands.

A.W.E.S.O.M.E.

Guiding Principle #2: You are a Subject Matter Expert

Early in my career, a producer I worked for told me the key to success in the entertainment business is to "fake it until you make it." Years later, I discovered this is also a motto used in twelve-step programs. The idea is that you immerse yourself into the project or program, and figure it out along the way. Your "faking it" is the self-realization that you don't know how to do it, but it is also the self-acknowledgment that you can figure it out.

Too often we focus on the first part: the fact that we don't know how to do something. Mishawn Nolan, an entertainment lawyer, intellectual property specialist, and partner at Nolan Heimann, describes this feeling in a powerful way:

> I think a lot of people have the fear of being a fraud, that when they get up and speak in front of the public, maybe it'll be exposed that they are not as much of an expert on the subject [as some may believe].

The second part, "the self-acknowledgment that you can figure it out," is an empowering shift in thinking. When you sincerely and whole-heartedly immerse yourself into a project, you practice *experiential learning*, which is mastering how to do something by actually doing it.

For example, you don't really learn how to swim by reading it in a book; you learn how to swim by doing it. You may read about the fundamentals of a proper swimming technique, but it is not until you engage in the act that you actually learn how to do it.

Being an experiential learner means you are building upon each experience, both good and bad, to become an expert. That expertise may be in baseball, knitting, relationships, accounting, writing, or any of a million things. The point is that experiences are learning tools to become more proficient.

That is not to say that you don't make mistakes at whatever the given task is, but as an experiential learner, you practice and become better.

Do you think every actor started out being brilliant the first time they read a script? Many in the film industry would testify with a "Heck, no!" They learned to build their craft— to take in the experience of a given mishap or success— and use it to become more of an expert.

You, too, are an expert in what you've done or are learning to do. It can be a skill, hobby, task, or relationship like parenting.

Mishawn believes it's important to focus on what you love:

> You will always feel confident in speaking about who you really are and not pretending to be something you're not. If you hate numbers, managing people, or

coming up with business plans, you're not going to do those business functions well. You're not going to devote the time necessary to grow in that area. It's really important to focus on the area that you love. You typically love to do things that you thrive in, that are authentic to you, that you had positive reinforcement in.

Your experiences and the knowledge you gain from them are incredibly valuable. What is simple and transparent to you, may not be to others. Fully embrace your skills and accomplishments. Here's an example.

The TV Newbie

Successful casting agent and TV producer, Ric Enriquez, recalls how he needed to shift the mindset of his expertise when he got his first job:

> When I was very young, I was putting together a resume. I took it to a service that writes up resumes for you, because I had no idea how to do that myself. I paid someone a hundred dollars, which was huge for me at the time.
>
> I don't remember her name, but she said, "You have a lot more experience than you think you do." She showed me how to think of what I did in the best terms, not in terms of lying, but "Look, you ran crews of people, so you can say you have management experience."

She taught me not to be intimidated when I started to apply for jobs. It changed me. It changed everything.

I took that mindset, where I always look to my strength, and coupled that with my innate ability to understand that in a job interview, they're looking for reassurance that you are the right candidate. I have talked my way into every job that I was unqualified for on paper, but knew I could do.

When I sat with my interviewer, who would be my future boss, I explained why I thought I could do it, and why my past experiences touched upon all the skills they needed. I reassured them I wasn't intimidated and was completely capable of doing the job. It made them feel comfortable in taking a chance on me. Because none of us are born doing what we do, we all have to do it at some point for the first time.

And like the resume writer told Ric, you too have more expertise than you might think. Your experience has taught you much more than you might acknowledge. Learn to embrace it. The world needs it.

Guiding Principle #3: You Instinctively Know

The phrase, "I don't know what to do" is a way of avoiding responsibility. The truth is, you instinctively know what to do. Your internal dialogue tells you.

A.W.E.S.O.M.E.

It's that voice inside that might say, "This isn't right," or "There's got to be another way," or "I shouldn't do this."

It's also that voice that says, "This is exactly what I need to do" or "This is right." It is knowing that the next action you take is what's best at this moment in time.

But, like in all conversations, do we listen?

For example, when I was that seventeen-year-old candidate out on the football field, I knew putting on the mask was a bad idea. Yet I still did it. Why? I was scared that I, myself, was not enough. On the other hand, at twenty-five years old, I left my home in Los Angeles, California, to help set up a TV show in Dallas, Texas. Why? I knew it would help build my career.

In both situations, I learned a lot about my internal dialogue and my instinct.

When you say to yourself, "I don't know what to do," what you're really saying is, "I am scared because I can't predict the result."

When you say, "This is right," you are affirming your confidence.

Listening to that voice inside is important. It shows up in your body and propels you into motion. It is the foundation for ambition—or lack of it.

The Guiding Principles

The Determined Agent

Talent agent and partner at WME Entertainment, Tim Curtis, had this kind of "knowing" and it proved to be a valuable asset to him.

> I knew the company I wanted to work for. I went to law school thinking that that would help get me in there, into the mailroom essentially, because that's how everybody starts.

> When I finished school, I bought a car and drove across country to Los Angeles. I went to that company, I called them, I emailed them, and I wrote them letters. I even sent the head of human resources flowers—and I couldn't get an interview. I couldn't get a return phone call. I couldn't get anything. I was blocked out of the company that I was so determined to work for.

> They used temps from one specific temp agency. I called the president there and said, "This is who I am, this is where I'm destined to work, and you put temps there. So put me in for one day and I promise you they will buy me from you. I promise you that I will perform enough to stay at this company."

> He had no idea who I was, but he appreciated that I put myself out there and called him. He gave me an opportunity and gave me a temp job at this company. It's the company I've worked at now for over twenty years.

A.W.E.S.O.M.E.

When you listen to your intuition—the inner voice that says "I know"—you not only build your confidence, you also create opportunities. You create action. Even if that action is a "mistake" or something that doesn't produce an immediate desired result, it gives you fuel and perspective on what to do—or not do—the next time you're presented with an opportunity.

When this knowing is combined with your creative being, you are powerful. You are the expert.

Connecting the Links

All three skills—your creative self, your expertise, and your instinctive knowing—are distinctly your own. They are based on the experience of you being you. Nobody else sees what you see and that is a remarkable thing to know. When you are in your true, wonderfully unique "you space," you are at maximum effectiveness.

When you operate with these three principles, you have the foundation to unleash the A.W.E.S.O.M.E. you.

SECTION II:

Surrender

CHAPTER 3

What's Fear Got to Do with It?

Public speaking is the number one fear in the world,
but it doesn't have to be yours.

It's natural to be scared when you speak in front of others.

Stop and think for a moment. When you step onto a stage in front of an audience or appear in front of a video camera with a message, what do you bring with you? Is it just you and your message? Or do you also bring baggage in the form of expectations, doubts, and unchecked fears?

It doesn't matter if it's a group of unknowns or a gathering of familiar faces. The mere act of putting yourself out there is unnerving. It's a naked, raw feeling. It's a choice to be vulnerable.

And fears manifest differently. You might feel inadequate when it comes to public speaking and do whatever you can to avoid being the center of attention. Or you might thrive on attention and are the first one to step up, volunteer, and take center stage.

So how can you get past your fear to stand up, speak out, and be heard?

You need to embrace your innate charisma and unleash your speaking potential. You already have the ability within you to delight and move an audience. In both subtle and earth-changing ways, you make a difference to those who hear and see you. All you have to do is fully immerse yourself into the message.

Surrender your notions of what makes a "good" speaker. Instead, focus on your purpose and become the message.

A.W.E.S.O.M.E.

Abandon expectations of how you should sound, look, and feel. The quest to control every aspect of a given situation—from the audience, to the environment, to every detail involved—is often your greatest saboteur. Your biggest enemy to being a radiant speaker just might be the person in the mirror: your fear-fighting self.

Whatever the case may be, insecurities are tricky. They are distinct and personal. What if you have a need for affirmation? The moment you don't get it, you feel empty. It's a fire that must remain lit, and if it burns out, you are without purpose. It leads you to do anything and everything to be "seen." Attention-seeking personalities appear in politics, in the media, and in personal space that includes family, friends, and colleagues.

When I campaigned to be student body treasurer in high school, I desperately wanted my classmates to validate me. "Jess, we like you. You are valuable." But that day when I spoke to them on the football field, I didn't show up as just me. I wasn't alone. Teasing from childhood classmates, disparaging comments from authority figures, and other hurtful past feelings joined me on that stage. They spoke louder than I did.

My fears controlled me.

This actually happens a lot. Fear and anxiety take over, and it does not matter who you are, how much money you make, or your place in society.

What's Fear Got to Do with It?

The Socialite

I've had the pleasure to work with some amazing personalities throughout my career. There have been actors, politicians, media personalities, influencers, and, of course, there have been the "everyday celebrities." The socialite was one of them.

A woman of means, she had everything she could ever dream of. She was a stay-at-home mom, lived in one of the most expensive areas in Northern California, and was held in high esteem in her community for her philanthropic efforts. She and her husband provided a privileged life for their children, including the best private schools. She worked tirelessly in the background so that her sons would be stars.

One day she was called upon to step from behind the scenes to the podium. Her younger son's high school asked her to make an introductory presentation to parents of the incoming freshman class. She was scared to death. I saw the fear in her eyes.

She breathed heavily and almost passed out every time she began to practice. She was so filled with fear that instead of embracing it, she tried to bury it. As a result, she became disconnected from her content, was stiff, and spoke in a monotone voice. At a time when she was supposed to make new parents feel welcomed, she turned distant and robotic.

However, there was one part of her speech that always made her cry, and that was when she thought about her son. She was his biggest fan. Since he was now in his senior year, when she reminisced about his freshman year, she couldn't help but get emotional.

At one point during the coaching process, she wanted to get rid of this portion of her presentation. When I asked why, she broke down in tears. She told me by acknowledging *what was,* she would have to now look at *what is...* that her son would soon be graduating and going away to college. This made her sad not only because he was going to leave, but also because it meant she didn't know what she was going to do next.

She gave everything to her family and was now being confronted with "What's next?" A question many of us face. We don't have to be like her, a person who is literally closing one chapter of her life and about to embark on a new one. You might be at a different crossroad, like "What am I going to say next in this pitch?" or "What should I do next to impress this client?"

Focusing on the "What's next?" question puts your mind into future thinking. That's unknown territory. It's a naturally scary place.

Instead, ask yourself, "What's in front of me right now?"

For the socialite, that's exactly what she needed to do.

What's Fear Got to Do with It?

She needed to release the emotion she bottled up about her son leaving and did so during one of our coaching sessions. Like a small water leak in a dam, it led to a much bigger flow of emotion that broke down the wall she had spent so much time building. She didn't want to show that volume of emotion during her talk, so she chose to bury it instead of deal with it.

In the end, she did release a few tears the afternoon of her presentation, but she stayed in the moment with her audience. Her fears did not control her. Instead, she learned how to use her emotion to enhance her message. She was a more effective speaker as a result.

The Quest to be Fearless

Fear is a powerful communication tool. It can limit us or catapult us as speakers.

It doesn't matter whether you are called to pitch a business, give a toast, or conduct a work presentation. There is a real fear to putting yourself out there. It's not just in some of us; even the most seasoned speakers deal with fear. Just ask two friends of mine, both of whom are professional speakers.

"I used to be terrified of public speaking. I literally would be shaking and feel like I was going to throw up. I would think, 'Oh my gosh, why am I doing this? I'm so worried and nervous; that means I shouldn't be a speaker.'"

> *– Julie Carrier, international professional speaker,*
> *author, and CEO of Girls Lead Worldwide*

"We're all swimming in a bucket-load of performance anxiety dictated by whomever we're performing for, whether it's parents, whether it's school, whether it's a company, whether it's Wall Street, you name it. We're all asked to perform. As soon as that 'performance' word comes into my thinking, I'm like, 'Oh, I better be good.'"

> *– Rick Tamlyn, author, speaker,*
> *and creator of The Bigger Game*

Ever feel like Julie or Rick?

Julie delivers empowering messages to girls and teens throughout the world. Rick challenges international audiences to play a bigger game. They both speak to small groups and to crowds of thousands. Regardless of the audience size, how they approach their personal fear is what makes a difference.

They embrace the fear.

Being "fearless" is a BIG concept that is unachievable. Trying to negate or conquer your fears creates contraction—you close your heart, get in your head, and question your gut. This leads many of us to act the way we believe others have acted to appear "fearless."

What's Fear Got to Do with It?

Take a look at boys on the playground. There always seems to be that one who puffs up his chest, flexes his muscles, and says, "Look at how strong I am!" He is mirroring what he's seen either directly by older kids and adults or through images in the media. He acts strong and his peers may even believe him—but is he?

In what ways do you do this? How often does your fear prompt you into acting? Are you like me and countless others who become great pretenders?

In our pursuit to be fearless speakers, we become less enabled communicators. Our head takes control of our heart and gut, so we abandon our emotions and intuition. As a result, we are less effective.

Fear is fuel. It informs your emotions and intuition, two keys elements that allow you to relate and connect to your innermost self. When you try to control fear, you squelch these parts of yourself. Every time you try to be "bigger" than your fear or eliminate it, you surrender your power to it.

You become reactive. You are not really in control, but somehow believe you are.

As a result, you lose an essential part of your personal power. Your energy gets depleted and you disconnect yourself from others.

Deep inside, you know that trying to control fear does not

serve you. So the challenge is not to beat it, but to own it. Respect it. And learn how to use it.

Becoming FearFULL

Imagine if you chose to be *fearFULL*—or FULL of FEAR. Embracing your fears keeps you connected to your emotions. It empowers that true expressive part of yourself, that place where your personality thrives, where you laugh, smile, cry, scream, dance, seduce, and create all kinds of powerful expressions of yourself.

Leaning into your emotions—not away from them— enables you to be vulnerable. By being vulnerable, you rely on your own personal strength. You explore how to best express yourself and become a strong speaker, not a strong pretender.

Julie Carrier says there's a science to this kind of thinking.

> My background in public speaking is based in neuroscience. When you're in a new situation, and particularly one in public, the body knows that that is a new type of environment. In order to help you succeed, it actually releases additional chemicals like cortisol and a lot of neurotransmitters that help to make sure you're super awake, focused, and amped up, ready to perform.

What's Fear Got to Do with It?

What people are interpreting as nervousness is actually just the extra energy the body's giving that person to succeed. Because they've never been taught how to interpret it, it becomes a crippling effect instead of an enhancing effect. The worst thing to tell somebody when he or she is trying to perform, give a speech, or present something is to "calm down." The sympathetic nervous system is all about making sure that you are super primed and ready to succeed in this new situation.

Julie practices this mindset whenever she speaks.

I learned, that "Oh my gosh, this is the way the body works!" Every time I go to give a speech now, I always tell myself, "You know what? Rather than being nervous, I'm actually really excited and my body's giving me the extra energy I need to succeed."

Nervousness and excitement show up in the body in exactly the same way. Your blood is flowing, your heart is racing, and your body just wants to move. The difference is how you interpret this feeling.

Are you nervous or excited? The label you choose makes a big difference.

I get that "nervous" feeling every time I coach a new client, teach a new class, or draft a new blog. At moments like these, my body is telling me two things: (1) whatever I am doing right now is important, and (2) it requires a lot from me.

A.W.E.S.O.M.E.

What Does It Require?

The idea that "it requires a lot from me" is intimidating. Insecurities, negative self-talk, and doubt can paralyze you when you keep asking, "Am I good enough? Can I do this? What will happen if...?"

And that's the moment when your internal dialogue needs to shift.

What is "required of me" you already have. Embrace the guiding principle: "I am a subject matter expert."

You already have the knowledge, the skills, and the answers. Now, you are just being called to look within, to acknowledge these gifts you have spent a lifetime building.

At this point, many people start spinning in their heads. The idea that "whatever I am doing right now is important" is already intimidating. Add to that your role as subject matter expert—you are the one who will provide the answer or solution—and it becomes even more overwhelming.

You may be tempted to look outside of yourself for what to say or do. For example, you might pretend to be strong like the boys in the playground, wear a mask like a political candidate, or start over-rehearsing your message. Or you might go to the other extreme: shut down, lose your connection to fear, and subdue the nervous/excitement emotion that can be an asset to you.

What's Fear Got to Do with It?

You choose. Decide whether this fear is going to excite you or stop you. There are two streams of thought:

- "This is important. I have to take care of it. I don't know how. It's scary. I can't do it... Who has the answer?"

- "This is important. I have to take care of it. I don't know how. It's exciting. I can do it... I will find the answer."

Two of the guiding principles become useful when we are faced with this kind of fear: I am creative and instinctively know what to do.

For the socialite, the answer to what was important at her defining moment was to be there, as a sincere and loving parent for other moms and dads. The answer to "I need to take care of this" was doing exactly what she did—being an open and thoughtful presenter who connected to her audience as one of them.

You, too, are called to be a part of your audience. This includes being **fearFULL** and making the choice to be excited, not nervous.

A.W.E.S.O.M.E.

Lesson Learned

You are a perfectly imperfect person first, a speaker second.

Start by being the most connected and grounded person you can possibly be before you step on the stage, start your pitch, or speak. Show up exactly as you need to in that moment, and don't worry about the future outcome. Being in the present is what being A.W.E.S.O.M.E. is all about. Do that first, and you are well on your way to being a masterful and skillful speaker.

Summary

- It is natural to be scared in front of an audience. Even the most seasoned speakers get nervous.

- When you are nervous, your body is telling you two things: (1) what you're about to do is important, and (2) it requires thoughtful action.

- What you choose to do with emotion and energy once you start speaking *is* up to you. Embrace it as excitement and soar. Don't give into nervousness and skid to a halt.

- Being fearless is an unattainable goal. Being *fearFULL* allows your emotions and intuition to fuel and empower you.

Exercise

1. Identify an embarrassing moment in your life and how it impacted you. Think about a situation you would not normally share. Examples of the experience might be: dropping out of college, wearing a bad bridesmaid dress, or getting fired from a job. Find a picture that represents that experience; for example, a photo of your bridesmaid dress or former college.

2. Then write a paragraph on how you want to be perceived when you speak or do a presentation. Include the impression you want to make with audiences and what you hope they think about you when you are done speaking. What sort of feelings do you want to leave with them? Please be as specific as possible.

3. Compare the two and then write a half-page introduction of yourself. Integrate the embarrassing moment, keeping in mind the way you want to be perceived.

4. Read the introduction to someone you don't know.

5. Ask for feedback on how the embarrassing moment helped or hindered the way you want to come across.

6. When you admit and reveal something you are embarrassed about, how are you being *fearFULL*?

Call to Action

Choose to be *fearFULL*. Respect your fear and learn how to use it.

CHAPTER 4

The Audience is Listening

A true communicator is never alone.

In our digital age, human contact is more important than ever. Even with social media, online videos, images, emails, and video conferencing, we still need to foster a personal connection with others. Regardless of the environment or medium, you are addressing a real person with real needs and emotions. It is this human condition that successful speakers touch and speak to.

Yet in a room with a thousand listeners, some speakers don't know the audience exists. They are more focused on their delivery and agenda than they are on the people listening to them. Their talking points take precedence over the people who are listening to them.

Communication is a dynamic exchange. A good speaker engages in a dialogue, not a monologue. A successful message can only be delivered if he or she is speaking to the heart and mind of the listener. The audience is an equal and vital part of a keynote or presentation. Without addressing their needs, you might as well be speaking to yourself.

Professional speaker, Julie Carrier, encapsulates this idea quite well:

> Sometimes people think "public speaking" is just when you're in front of a large audience and you've got your microphone. The truth is any time you're in an environment where you're communicating a message, you're engaging in public speaking. The key is to

remember that public speaking is a conversation. If you realize that you're having a conversation with that person, that you care about them, and you get feedback from them—then that's the same thing.

The ultimate goal is that your audience hears you, as well as feels and experiences what you feel and experience. The rock star is one example of a speaker who was able to do just that.

The Rock Star

Emily and I met the rock star at our first public speaking workshop. He was a handsome, well-put-together, understated man who showed up in professional attire. A man of very few words, he expressed himself primarily with his eyes and smile. Even though he was kind-hearted, his reserved demeanor came across stiff and boring.

Did he have what it took to be a good speaker? He had a gentle, yet powerful voice. That first day he spoke about being a passionate person, however, he didn't embody it. He lacked that spark.

Little did we know, a fire of energy burned below the surface. Underneath this mild-mannered executive was a rock star! Literally. He was a bassist in a band, and a good one.

The Audience is Listening

We asked him to bring his bass guitar and perform for us on the second day of the workshop. The result was electric. The performer showed up and he lit up the room. He was magnetic.

Sharing his love of music and how he discovered it really allowed us to connect with him. He didn't just talk about his talent; he showed it. We guided him on how to integrate a small performance into a truly inspirational talk.

We are all artists. We all have the potential to express our passion in a way that takes an audience on a journey. You don't need to be a musician or actor to speak with the passion of an artist. You can be a doctor, a restaurant owner, or a student, and express yourself in a masterful and artistic way.

Begin by embracing your inner passion, that special something only you have. Foster it, and then share it in a way that connects to and potentially transforms your audience.

Remember, no one can tell your story except you.

Inform and Connect to Your Audience

Effective speakers know that purposeful communication has two components: *information* and *connection*. These two elements come into play every time you address an audience, whether it is an audience of one or of many. You want to meet and dance (or connect) with them *where they are* and, at the same time, give them something they did not have before. This could be a unique point of view, new information, or a different way of looking at a subject.

The rock star, for example, connected with his audience through his music and it informed them about his passion.

Information might take the form of sharing your expertise, your opinion, or product with another. Your unique experience brings newness to the subject. The audience can learn from your message, be moved by it, and come away feeling connected to you. Connection is the bond you create with your audience. They respect you and relate to you because you engage them on a personal level.

You also reach an audience by understanding and connecting to what they value. These values vary from one audience to the next. For example, the best way to communicate with your boss is different from how you would communicate with a business colleague. Each of them cares about different results and has distinct expectations from you.

Everyone you meet—whether it is a boss, friend, or associate—has a specific role in your life. They each have their own agenda and personal goals for your relationship, just like you have with them.

The Audience is Listening

TV programming executive and producer, Loren Ruch, receives pitches for television shows. He then takes the best possibilities to his bosses and tries to sell them the idea. He knows each boss has a distinct perspective and, therefore, has to be approached differently. His advice is on how to gauge your message to your relationships:

> I study who I'm pitching to and I pitch the way that they want to hear it. You have to know the tone of the person that you're pitching to... you have to know the likes and dislikes of the person... you have to know the approach that they like. I pitch different things differently to different people in the company. I have one boss who's much more formal. I do a bullet-point presentation. I back it up with research. I make sure I spell-check. Then, I present it in a way that's nice, neat, and organized. I have another boss who wants the emotion: "I'm so excited about the show! I think this is going to work!" So, I can pitch the exact same project in two totally different ways, to try and get both of them on board. So, I think it's customizing it to the needs of the person or place that you're pitching to.

Learn how to identify the goals of others and you can optimize how you communicate with them for better mutual results. You can connect with them *where they are at* and inform them in a way that helps you both.

A.W.E.S.O.M.E.

Audience A.I.D.

When you identify the roles of people around you, it is an **A.I.D.** to your agenda and can help clarify and focus your message. **A.I.D.** is an acronym for three different types of audiences.

1. **Allies**. They respect and value what you have to offer. Using an online example, they are friends on Facebook or followers on Instagram. You keep them updated and rely on their feedback or likes. At work, they might be your colleagues. Your communication with them is familiar and less formal. They provide you with a sense of community.

2. **Influencers**. They are "in the know." Online, they have thousands of Twitter followers. In your childhood, this was the parent who convinced the stricter one to let you do what you wanted. Their stamp of approval is important. Your communication with them is strategic. They legitimize you and your work.

3. **Decision Makers**. They are definitive, yes-or-no people. Online, they are the eBay buyers. You try to maintain a good reputation with them and deliver on your promises. In business, they are clients. At work, he or she may be your boss. Your communication with them is deliberate and direct. You pitch to them. They determine the results.

The Audience is Listening

Examining these people, their roles, and their reason for listening to you, is a great place to start when you are preparing your presentation. It will add a sense of clarity to your agenda and potentially ease your anxiety when you speak.

When I did my campaign speech for student body treasurer, I did not approach it with the right audience in mind. I wanted my classmates to affirm me and, as a result, I gave them the power to be "decision makers" for my self-esteem. In reality, certain members of that audience may have been influencers, but all of them could have been allies. Looking at them more carefully would have helped my speech.

How often do you look at your audience as decision makers? Do you give them the responsibility as a decision maker to determine your value as a friend, expert, or leader? Too many times, we give our audience this burden. We look to them to decide our worthiness. In reality, no one should decide your worthiness but you.

How do you take the burden off your audience — and step into the role as subject matter expert?

Identify your relationship with your audience ahead of time. Know whether he/she/they are allies, influencers or decision makers. This will inform the way you approach each of them. This will facilitate the words you use, the stories you tell, and the mediums you might use.

A.W.E.S.O.M.E.

Determining in advance the best way to connect with them is a powerful tool when it comes to speaking to them.

Think of A.I.D. as a helpful arrow. It points and guides you on how to approach a specific audience. Let's break this down more by examining the approach that might be most effective with each of these distinct audiences.

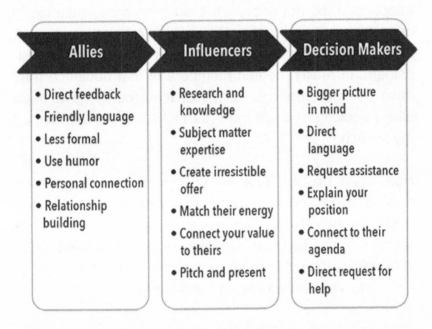

Allies	Influencers	Decision Makers
• Direct feedback • Friendly language • Less formal • Use humor • Personal connection • Relationship building	• Research and knowledge • Subject matter expertise • Create irresistible offer • Match their energy • Connect your value to theirs • Pitch and present	• Bigger picture in mind • Direct language • Request assistance • Explain your position • Connect to their agenda • Direct request for help

Better understanding of your audience allows you to be more effective with them because you can be precise with your communication. You don't have to waste time and words while figuring out where they are coming from. And even if you have to pivot during your talk, it is far easier to change course than it is to start over.

The Audience is Listening

When you are precise and purposeful with your communication approach, you create influence. You assure your audience that you are not going to waste their time and they learn to trust you. You "know them" and their needs.

With each of these three audiences—allies, influencers, and decision makers—you are building relationships. Understanding the predisposition of these quintessential relationships allows you to effectively engage and connect with them. As a speaker, when you are in tune with their needs and purpose, your message resonates and relationships flourish.

A.W.E.S.O.M.E.

Lesson Learned

There is no need to pretend. Express yourself and your artistry authentically and the audience will embrace you.

There are different types of audiences. They each have a role. Knowing how to approach them, what words to use when you speak to them, and what they value allows you to better connect with them in a genuine and sincere way. Show them your artistry, your expertise, and take them on a journey.

Summary

- Communication is a dynamic exchange. An effecttive speaker engages in a dialogue, not a monologue.

- Know the relationship with your audience: are they allies, influencers, or decision makers?

- Understand what your audience needs from you, then you can better communicate with them.

- We are all artists. We all have the potential to express our expertise, our gift, our passion in a way that takes the audience on a guided journey.

Exercise

Take a moment to consider your artistry. How do you express it? Is it something you share with others or keep only to yourself? Write down three ways your expertise may benefit others. Then prepare a two-minute presentation on your expertise and its benefits. Remember to find a way to showcase your expertise or artistry. Afterward, give this presentation to an audience of two or more friends.

Call to Action

Be bold enough to share your artistry with the world around you. Release your enchanting, expressive power.

CHAPTER 5

The Powerful Dialogue Within

You are more powerful than you think.

Too often I hear people say, "I am not good enough."

"I am not captivating enough... interesting enough... or charismatic enough... to be a good speaker."

The notion of not being enough, whatever the reason, gives many people an out. It gives them permission not to try.

This is usually followed up by a self-defeating dispensation such as: "That's just the way I am." While there is great strength in understanding that statement, it does not have to limit your potential. For example, being shy doesn't mean that it's "Just the way you are."

I work with people to help build their confidence so they can show up and speak about *who they are* and their irresistible offer with clarity and conviction. This requires them to go beyond their own limited thinking. Confidence starts first with an examination of internal dialogue.

That's why the three guiding principles outlined in Chapter 2 are so important. These principles help combat negative self-talk. When you embrace that you are creative, skillful, and instinctive (the three guiding principles), you begin to own your personal power.

The challenge is for you to transform any critical self-talk you might have, such as "I am not good enough" or "That's just the way I am." Instead, ask yourself to show up as your best self.

A.W.E.S.O.M.E.

When you reconstruct your internal dialogue, you build up your confidence. This allows you to show up in a remarkable way. As discussed in my book, *Everyday Celebrity*, the 3 Cs—"Clarity, Confidence and Charisma"—work together for more effective communication.

In the pursuit of better public speaking, the goal is to get clear about your message, stand up confidently as the "best me possible," and speak with your own inherent natural charisma.

Charisma is your consistent and committed style of self-expression. It is based on your authentic and unique personality characteristics. Being charismatic does not require you to be an extrovert. How you show up as your best self—be it quietly or loudly—is all that matters.

Likewise, addressing an audience does not require you to be an extrovert. In fact, fairly often, the quieter, gentler forces are the most powerful.

Take a look at the rock star as an example. He had a calm demeanor. He was expressive through his music. That was his expertise. I am not advocating that you become a musician or a performer in order to express yourself. Rather, cultivate the expert within and listen to your inner self-talk.

Being "at my best" is not an easy task. Past failures, trials, and hurts interfere. A tenacious internal voice may hold us back, trapping us in self-doubt.

The Powerful Dialogue Within

Many of us also suffer from another self-defeating belief: "I need to be perfect." I subscribed to this self-sabotaging message for years. I tried to present a perfect version of what I thought I should be. It was an unrealistic and unreachable goal.

Much of what I thought I should be, I couldn't be. The crusade exhausted me.

The following simple, yet empowering, statement changed my life. It is a personal mantra taught to me by a friend:

**"I am going to show up exactly
as I need to be in this moment."**

When you say this to yourself, you are able to show up in that given situation as the best version of yourself, knowing your power.

No longer are you held captive by the notion, "I am not good enough," or "This is just how I am." Nor do you have to fall into the perfectionist trap.

You are free to experiment. You are free to show up in context, not in expectation.

Mantras are powerful tools, especially when it comes to public speaking. The internal dialogue you have with yourself shows up in how you communicate out loud.

A.W.E.S.O.M.E.

Personal Power Requires Work

When your inner light shines and you allow others to see it, you embrace your personal power. You know with certainty there is something special that only you can offer to the world. This is what I've been referencing as your *irresistible offer*. And when you speak about this gift and bring awareness to it, your personal power takes flight.

This is confidence. It may feel uncomfortable because to many of us, it feels like bragging. If you can accept that uncomfortable feeling, it can ultimately make you a stronger speaker.

Like the introvert who might be scared to speak in front of a crowd, try something that challenges you. Be bold.

Reality TV casting director and producer, Jill Bandemer, has the following advice for the inexperienced, cautious speaker:

> I think for those of us who love to talk or were born talkers, speaking comes easily. For other people, social awkwardness or anxiety holds them back. When I do casting interviews, I don't push the interviewee too hard, but I do encourage them to express their thoughts completely, urging them to "say it again and say this." I encourage them to speak in full sentences.

Jill speaks to hundreds of potential reality TV stars every

week. She weeds out the best speakers or potential stars, but also encourages those who may not articulate well to do better.

Likewise, Ric Enriquez, casting director, producer and show creator, has this to say about how others support a speaker:

> The thing we often tell actors is know that when you walk into a room, everyone wants you to succeed because it makes our jobs easier if you're good. You have to not add pressure to yourself.

Indeed. Your audience is cheering for you. The importance of this alliance cannot be overstated. At the very least, they want to be comfortable themselves, which they can only be if you are. They are investing their time because they hope you will give them something they want or need. They are not sitting there hoping you'll fail. See them as friends, not judges. And while they want you to be your best, that doesn't mean you have to be perfect. Your greater power lies in being relatable.

On-camera pop culture expert and TV programming executive, Brian Balthazar, who knows what it is like to be on both sides of the camera, says to just let go.

> Once I let go of the idea that I had to deliver everything perfectly, I was okay. There's something inspirational about seeing someone who has perfect delivery, but

there's also something really relatable about someone who's very conversational and gets a feeling across. It may not be delivered in the perfect way, but you're like, "Okay, I can relate to that. I'm not perfect either." It's about being relaxed, being comfortable, and not being so over-prepared that you're unable to react to things that are happening around you.

This is the foundation of the mantra, "I am going to show up exactly as I need to in this moment."

Being relatable is a skill. It requires vulnerability. We all have the power to decide what we personally want to reveal about ourselves. Hold onto that personal part of yourself that makes you feel safe and comfortable. At the same time, challenge yourself to reveal personal details. You are more compelling when others can relate to you.

Take a look at one social media influencer's challenge to find this balance.

The Social Media Influencer

A fashion model and former beauty pageant contestant, this Instagram star was poised. She knew exactly what her audience wanted to see from her and delivered it in her posts. She offered inside access to photo shoots and exotic locations. But as her popularity grew, her fans wanted to know more about her, to look inside the personal life of the persona they had grown to admire.

The Powerful Dialogue Within

She wasn't self-revealing at all. Early in her career, she endured a very tumultuous and public breakup with another star and, as result, chose not to share anything personal from that point forward. She didn't talk about her family or whom she was dating. She aimed to shield herself from public scrutiny. Ironically, at the same time, she also ran a business fueled by public perception—as a personality brand in social media.

People criticized her for being too private. They labeled her snotty and "too good" to be real. They stereotyped her as a self-centered "beauty queen." They called her shallow and vapid. She was unfairly characterized and this not only hurt her personally, it impacted her professionally.

Keylee Sanders, a fashion stylist and on-air host who is a former beauty pageant contestant herself, has this to say about the preconceived notions of beauty and brains:

> They're called "beauty pageants" for a reason. You've got to be okay with that … but, if you've watched one, you'll know there's more than beauty that matters. I won based on my interview, and that's something that I'm very proud of.

Likewise, the Instagram star was a smart, articulate individual. This worked for her and against her when it came to dealing publicly with her followers. She didn't want to have to prove herself or fight against the beauty stereotype.

A.W.E.S.O.M.E.

Have you ever felt the same way?

Stereotypes exist in all fields. For example, stereotypically, engineers lack interpersonal social skills, and rich people are self-absorbed. We all face certain preconceived notions ascribed to us from others. I have yet to meet anyone who hasn't faced some sort of prejudgment.

It's key not to be or play the victim. You don't need to prove yourself. You also don't need to protect yourself to the point that you don't reveal what makes you unique and irresistible. In fact, when you share your relatable qualities, you affirm your personal power and challenge your audience's stereotypical notions. While it may or may not change their ultimate thinking, it allows you to show up in that moment exactly as who you are—not as someone you think they want to see or you believe you should be.

The Instagram star ultimately chose to become more self-revealing, but was selective in what she shared in her posts. For example, she shared her love of dogs, talked about what it felt like to struggle at school, and how she looked forward to becoming a mom one day. She understood she was going to be criticized whether she shared something personal or not, so the effort to protect herself was a futile one. She modified her approach and it proved to be beneficial.

While you may not be a social media star like the one I worked with, you can't help but be seen. We are all under a social media and personal microscope. What you select to share about yourself and your life, however, is a choice you make.

Revealing Who You Are

There are three layers to your public identity. You choose what is in each layer and how much of it to share—or keep closed off—from others. They are:

1. *Core Self*, where you keep your most intimate fears and feelings. You might only share this part of yourself with a dear friend, spouse, or close family member.

2. *Expert Self*, where you share data about your passion or expertise.

3. *Personable Self*, where you share certain thoughts and emotions you are comfortable revealing in public.

Think of it this way. Your core self is at the center of your being. The next intimate layer is what you decide to personally reveal about yourself. The most outer layer is your expertise or passion. What you choose to reveal in each of these layers indicates how open or closed you are publicly, and how relatable you are to others.

A.W.E.S.O.M.E.

Guarded individuals keep all three of these elements hidden and closed off to others. As a result, the audience cannot relate or connect to them (Diagrams 5A and 5B).

Informed individuals share their passion and expertise with others. As a result, they allow audiences into their world (Diagrams 5C and 5D).

Open individuals are the most self-revealing individuals. They allow others to see their expertise, as well as some emotion and feelings. They are the most connected to their audiences (Diagrams 5E and 5F).

Diagram 5A

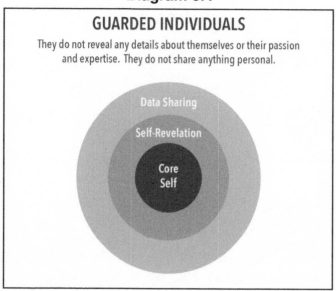

GUARDED INDIVIDUALS

They do not reveal any details about themselves or their passion and expertise. They do not share anything personal.

Diagram 5B

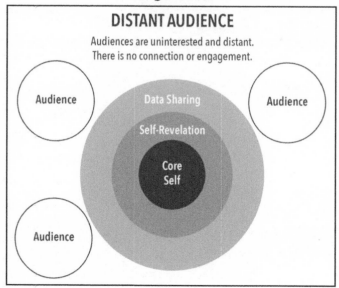

DISTANT AUDIENCE

Audiences are uninterested and distant.
There is no connection or engagement.

A.W.E.S.O.M.E.

Diagram 5C

INFORMED INDIVIDUALS

They share data or information about their passion and expertise,
but do not share or reveal personal feelings or emotions.

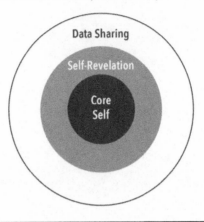

Diagram 5D

AN INFORMED AUDIENCE

The audience is more informed. They might learn something new or
have questions answered that were previously unknown.

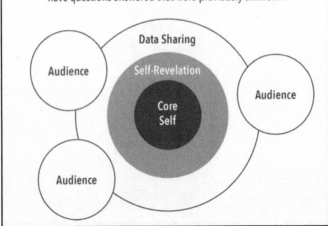

The Powerful Dialogue Within

Diagram 5E

OPEN INDIVIDUALS

They are vulnerable. They share information about their passion
and are self-revealing about feelings and emotions.

Data Sharing

Self-Revelation

Core
Self

Diagram 5F

CONNECTED AUDIENCE

The audience is connected to the speaker and his or her passion.
They embrace the speakers as imperfect, but powerful people.

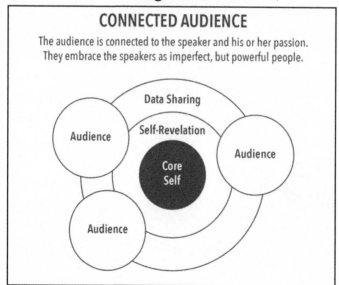

Data Sharing

Self-Revelation

Audience

Audience

Core
Self

Audience

Being self-revealing is not an all-or-nothing situation. You choose the degree to which you share yourself. Take a look at diagrams 5G and 5H. You have freedom on how deeply you want others to experience you, ranging from slightly open to fully vulnerable.

Diagram 5G

Diagram 5H

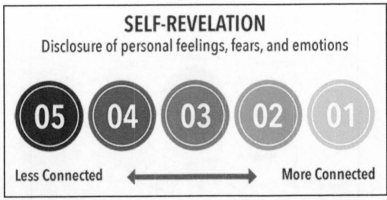

The Powerful Dialogue Within

Like the Instagram star, you are in control of how much you choose to open up to your audience. Originally, she was at Level 2 for information sharing and a Level 5 in self-revelation. She shared her expertise with her followers, but they wanted more. When she changed her level of self-revelation, even just a little bit to Level 3, she created a shift. Her followers, or audiences, began to relate to her on a more personal level. She became more deeply connected to them and her influence grew.

Where do you fall in these diagrams? Can you challenge yourself to be more open, more revealing? The choice is yours. The more you experiment and try, the better informed you become about your relatability.

Lesson Learned

You are more than enough. You have all the power to show up exactly as you need to in any given moment.

Self-defeating dialogue about your personal value impacts the way you communicate with others. But there is no need to pretend or try to be perfect. Knowing what feelings and/or opinions you want to keep to yourself and what you're willing to share with others is part of your personal power as a speaker.

Summary

- "I am not good enough" and "That's just how I am" are self-sabotaging beliefs.

- You are so much more powerful than you think.

- Perfectionism is a no-win and frustrating pro-position.

- You choose what to reveal about yourself and the degree to which you do it. You can be a guarded, informed, or open individual.

Exercise

Examine the previous diagrams (5A–5F) and honestly place yourself in one of the categories. Are you a guarded, informed, or open individual? Next, measure yourself from 1-5 on the data sharing and personal revealing categories. Does this work for you and your goals? If not, what measures work for you and what steps are required to get you there?

Call to Action

Learn to use mantras as part of your call to action to be a better speaker. Start with the mantra, *"I am going to show up exactly as I need to in this moment."*

QUOTABLE MENTIONS ON SURRENDERING

The following are additional thoughts and advice about fear and perfectionism. What entertainment professionals say about...

FEAR OF PUBLIC SPEAKING

"It's the closest we get to being naked in public. It's exposing your frailties."

- Ric Enriquez,
  Casting Director
  and Producer

"Claiming your opinion, something that you believe in, is a little scary. We are used to living in a world where you're trying to accommodate everybody."

- Loren Ruch,
  Programming Executive
  and Producer

"I think it's people's fear of looking stupid."

- Jill Bandemer,
  Reality TV Casting
  Director

OVERCOMING FEAR

"Terrified to speak up in company brainstorming sessions? Volunteer to lead the next one! When we push past our fear, we can focus on our own inner growth."

- Jess Weiner,
  Speaker, Author,
  and Actionist

"The more you feel comfortable with your messaging, the more you practice, the more it flows off your tongue like it's just something that's completely normal for you."

- Julie Carrier,
  Professional Speaker

"The number one rule in publicity is: not everyone's going to like you and not everyone's going to buy in to what you're selling."

- Amy Prenner,
  Entertainment Publicist

PERFECTIONISM

"The fear of not being perfect... the truth is, you won't be."

- Brian Balthazar,
  TV Executive and
  Media Personality

"I can't tell you one person that started perfect. I can tell you lots of people who worked hard and did the things they needed to do to become well-spoken."

- Sharon Hashimoto,
  Editor and Director

"We're all just human beings trying to figure out our place in the world."

- Shahnti Olcese Brook,
  Celebrity Booker,
  Producer, and Manager

SECTION III:

The A.W.E.S.O.M.E. You

CHAPTER 6
Aligned

Words don't communicate. You do.

When you let go of expectations and notions of how you should be, you liberate your innate star quality. It's that internal light that, when lit, you see it, others are drawn to it, and the world embraces it.

You don't have to look too far to find this light. Often, the secret is to step out of your own way. Don't let fear hold you back. Seize the moment to shine and deliver your irresistible offer with confidence and ease.

The power is within you if you. It is in your thoughts, your emotions, and in your intuition. When all three of these parts of yourself are in alignment—the thoughts in your head, the emotions in your heart, and the intuition in your gut—you begin to unlock the A.W.E.S.O.M.E. you.

The first step in this journey is to examine how you experience the world.

Speaking is an Experience

We experience the world as interactive individuals. We are not alone, operating as sole proprietors in an existence without some sort of interaction. We interact in many different ways, with people, surroundings, and mechanisms that help us function. The way we interact with all of these starts with the value and meaning we give them.

A.W.E.S.O.M.E.

For example, we interact with our moms in a certain way based on our love for them. We interact with the environment based on our regard for natural resources. But what about other mechanisms that help us experience the world around us?

Let's briefly look at three of them.

Music entertains us. Time schedules us. Food fuels us. All of these are devices that literally and figuratively move us in some way. Music can transform our moods or get our bodies on the dance floor. Time tells us when we need to do something or where we need to be. Food gives our bodies energy or moves us to try new delights.

We interact with these "things" and they help us experience our world in a certain way. Our experience is based on the meaning and value they have for us. For example, if you value being prompt, you have a close relationship to time, or if you value being fit, you choose to eat certain foods.

Speaking, likewise, is an interactive experience. It is a mechanism that helps you inform and connect with an audience. It can be an audience of one or of many.

As described in *Everyday Celebrity*, the interactive experience moves in a cycle.

Aligned

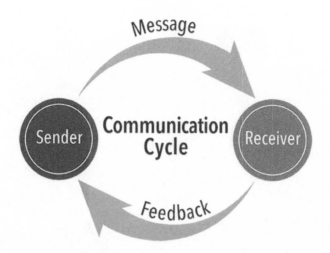

At times, the interactive experience is interrupted. Interference may occur for a myriad of reasons, such as background noise, reluctant audiences who are closed off to new ideas, or the speaker's singular approach because he or she is not fully engaged in the feedback. This often happens when the speaker is performing a monologue, or is merely focused on presenting an idea.

Communication Disruption

An effective speaker is fully engaged in feedback with the audience and is aware of potential interference in the communication cycle. This interference is called "static."

A.W.E.S.O.M.E.

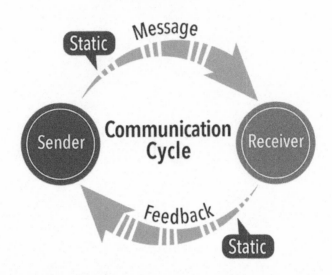

Think of static as your cell phone dropping your call, that moment when you can no longer hear the other person and you say, "Hello, hello, can you hear me?" The cell phone conversation experienced a disruption and the static prompts you to take some sort of action in order to see if the person on the other end is still listening.

Similarly, audience feedback makes a speaker aware of literal and figurative static. For example, when the audience looks uninterested or confused, this may be due to something mechanical, like poor microphone audio. Or their reaction might indicate the content does not flow, that the points are disjointed and somehow you as a speaker have lost your way. In either case, a successful speaker recognizes the disruption in the communication cycle and pivots accordingly.

Aligned

A speaker is not merely delivering a message; he or she is navigating an experience. This requires a full and comprehensive connection to the audience. It requires the speaker to be in alignment.

Alignment happens when your head, heart, and gut all work together in unison to deliver a message and experience. The speaker is called to use feelings and intuition, not words alone.

Here's an example of such an aligned speaker.

The Singer

The singer submitted her video to the very first AWESOME TALK. Initially, Emily and I were not overly impressed. She was an absolutely gorgeous model. A seemingly wonderful asset, physical beauty can also form a bias that a speaker must combat. Physical beauty can be a form of static.

For us, that was not the issue. But something was missing.

We knew she possessed a burning, shining light within, but it was barely visible on tape. Instinctively, Emily and I knew there was something more and we wanted to expose it.

She was a singer, and while she mentioned that briefly during her video, she didn't really highlight it. Maybe she felt it wasn't relevant. Maybe she wanted to be seen as something more than just a singer. Whatever her reason, she chose not to share one of her greatest gifts. She consciously made a choice to hold back.

As we began to work with her, she decided to share more of her gift. She did this initially by integrating a video of her singing into her talk. And while it was a lovely idea, it still fell short of compelling.

She chose to talk about her gift, not reveal it. This happens in many different ways. For example, have you been on a date when someone says, "I am really funny," but doesn't come across funny? Or at a job interview, someone says, "I am a team player," but doesn't share any examples?

While that person may, in fact, be funny or a team player, saying it isn't as poignant as showing it. Being funny is what creates impact. Revealing a story about when you were a team player is what showcases it.

Don't talk about your gift. Be the gift.

During one of our sessions, we encouraged the singer to sing. At first, she resisted. Her reasons: it was scary, her songs were full of emotion, she wanted it to be perfect, and didn't want to be judged if she made a mistake. All of these were valid fears.

Fear is something every speaker must face. You don't have to be a singer to experience these same doubts. But

Aligned

what you do with your doubts and fears is vital to your success.

A metamorphosis occurred when she chose to be *fearFULL*. Yes, she made a couple of mistakes. She cried. It wasn't "perfect." But it was, in fact, perfect for that situation. Connecting more deeply to her emotions, she embodied a message of love—the theme of her presentation.

Her talk was about her mom, the support her mom had given her through the years, and how this made her a powerful and loving person. She also told this story as a means to inspire others to embrace love in their lives.

By sharing your gift live and in person, you become the thriving example of your message.

The night of the event, she started out her talk with a heartfelt song. She set the mood for the audience, combating whatever static might be in the room, and proceeded to take those she engaged on a journey.

She became the message. She integrated her words (head), her feelings (heart), and her intuition (gut). She was aligned.

A.W.E.S.O.M.E.

Words Alone are not Enough

Your message is so much more than words. What drives it home are your emotions and intuition. When they are fused together with your words and expressed in unison, your message takes on a completely different form.

You communicate more effectively because you embody the message. You interact with your audience and create an experience for them.

In the same regard, when your words are left alone to speak for themselves, you risk not having true impact. You may still get across some information, but you may not connect with your listeners. Sharing information or data is only half the communication equation. Be purposeful with your message: share information and connect to those who are giving you their time and attention.

Emotion is easily explained. We all have feelings. Some of us may hold them back or deny them, but they are, nonetheless, part of us. And even if feelings are overwhelming, as in the case of the singer, when we integrate them into our communication, we are far more expressive and effective. They live in our hearts.

Intuition, on the other hand, requires more explanation. Intuition is your internal voice that knows what to do right here, right now. When cultivated, that voice guides the journey you take with your audience. It's like a compass. It is "knowing" what is required of you to be most effective.

Aligned

In Western culture, we refer to this "knowing" or intuition as a "gut feeling." Yet, often, we don't listen to it, even if we get a sinking feeling in our stomach.

Intuition informs you when to speak softly, when to add lightness such as laughter to a stressful situation, or when to be bold and direct with someone. We learn it as children. We assess when to ask our parents for permission to do something, when to tell our friends they did us wrong, or how far we can push our teacher.

Somewhere along the way, however, we also learn to suppress our intuition. As a result, we too often ignore our gut feeling as adults.

When we are connected to our intuition, we are better able to read the circumstance, relationship, or audience and take action based on what we are experiencing. It is the embodiment of the mantra, "I will show up exactly as I need to in this moment."

The audience knows if and when you show up aligned. They can see it and they can feel it. My colleague, media producer, celebrity booker and friend, Shahnti Olcese Brook, describes this when she is looking to book someone for a TV show or podcast:

> I have a gut or intuitive feeling when I'm watching someone. Whether I feel "That just isn't going to work," or "I just absolutely love that," I try to see if they are

having a good time. Do they look happy? Or do they look uncomfortable? It's all these different elements at the same time. I think, "That was awesome" or "That was so painful." And it affects my decision to book them.

Alignment in Action

When your mind, body, and gut are in symphony together, you create music like the singer and captivate your audience. When these three parts of your being are in sync, you know it. The audience experiences it.

How do you get there? It starts with awareness that you are more than just the words you use. You communicate with your entire being. You are a medium of expression.

The biggest key to communicating with your entire being is to foster your intuition. Your intuition is core to Guiding Principle #3: *"You instinctively know."* When nurtured, it is an incredibly valuable asset. Successful speakers in any platform know this to be true.

As award-winning producer Shahnti Olcese Brook describes, it is truly a valuable asset in and out of the entertainment business.

It is so important to trust your gut. If you feel like something isn't working, don't force it! Don't put the square peg into the round hole. Trusting your intuition is sometimes so much smarter than any other possible thing that you can do. There is a "ding" in our head, sort of like, "Hello! Hello!" Listen to it!

A.W.E.S.O.M.E.

Lesson Learned

When your mind, heart, and gut work in unison, you can fully express who you are and your irresistible offer. You are aligned. You are powerful. Too often, we rely only on words (or our mind) to convey messages. When we do that, we are less effective because we are not using our entire being to communicate. Trust your emotions and intuition. They are part of Guiding Principle #3: *You instinctively know*. Allow yourself to be fully expressive because what you feel in your heart and gut are eminently useful.

Summary

- Speaking is an interactive experience.

- Alignment happens when your entire expressive self—your ideas, emotion, and intuition—work together to communicate and deliver a message.

- In Western culture, we refer to intuition as a "gut feeling," yet we don't listen to it. Don't doubt your internal "knowing." Foster it.

- When you are connected to your intuition, you are better able to read the interactive communication experience and take action based on what you're experiencing.

Exercise

It's time to watch a new TV show or web series that you're unfamiliar with and have never seen before. Pick a random scene and watch it two times. The first time, play it without sound. Take notes on what you are experiencing, such as the characters, the environment, the situation, and emotions involved in the scene. What do your observations tell you?

Then watch it a second time with sound and compare the two. What did you already know from the first experience? What did your intuition tell you? What emotions did you experience? Then compare: how did the words in the second viewing confirm or negate your "knowing?" You might be surprised.

Call to Action

Express yourself with your entire being. Pay special attention to your emotions and intuition because they are the key to powerful presence.

Practice the mantra, *"I am aligned. I use my words, emotions, and intuition to fully express myself."*

CHAPTER 7
Wired

*It doesn't matter how much you prepare for a talk.
If you haven't created the right environment,
the audience won't hear you.*

Alignment occurs when you use all parts of your expressive self to communicate—your words, your emotions, and your intuition. When your head, heart, and gut work in unison, you become a better speaker. You know with every fiber of your being that what you are sharing is valuable. You have a greater sense of what to do in a given situation because you trust your intuition and worry less about being scared.

When your words, emotions, and intuition are connected, you become the message.

Connection

You must first be aligned within yourself before you can relate to others.

As a speaker, you take your audience on a journey. You are the guide of a communication experience. The audience gives you their time and attention—even if it's just for a moment—because they believe what you're about to say is relevant. Your knowledge, expertise, humor—whatever it is—is important for them at that moment. They trust you to give them something in this experience in exchange for their time and attention.

It's important to deliver something the audience values. Speakers who lose sight of this squander a precious opportunity.

A.W.E.S.O.M.E.

It's not about you, the speaker. It's about the audience and the experience you guide them through. You are providing a service. This perspective is key because you are a medium through which they receive some sort of information, insight, laughter or other meaningful message.

Yes, you, the speaker, are the most important medium in any public speaking situation. What you do, say, and emote are always more important than the stats on your PowerPoint or cute videos you use in your presentation. You are a living, breathing medium that needs to connect to your audience because they look to you as a guide or leader.

What you give the audience is paramount to public speaking. Get to know them, and make sure to be one among them. Ask yourself:

- How am I linked to this audience?
- What do they value?
- What do I have that they want?
- How might they best receive my message?
- Is it the right moment to engage them?

Entertainment publicists know "how to feel the room" or gauge the appropriate time to pitch a story. Their jobs depend on it. They are responsible for the reputation of high-profile clients, and they must skillfully navigate what to say and when to say it. Amy Prenner, President of the Prenner Group in Los Angeles, describes the right approach:

> There are two things that are really important. Number one is to know your audience. If it's a broadcast television segment that we're trying to secure, we need to find out, "What does [the journalist or producer] *Sally Smith* like? Does she like feel-good stories? Charity stories? Does she like celebrity dating stories?"

> And the second thing is... to follow the news cycles. If there's a shooting and fifty people were killed, don't pitch somebody. Take a beat. Wait.

> You have to be really sensitive to what's around you. And then when you are ready to do that kind of outreach, see where you can tie things in to make it more of a universal pitch as opposed to something that doesn't really have to do with anything. See where you can connect the dots.

Connecting the dots is so important when it comes to public speaking. Those dots include you, your message, the audience, the circumstance and so much more. Many elements play into the communication experience and a good public speaker is wired to these different components.

A.W.E.S.O.M.E.

Being wired means you are taking into account the total experience: the context, physical environment, mediums at your disposal, and purpose of the situation.

The Radio DJ

The radio DJ provides an excellent study on what it means to be wired. When she first submitted her video to the AWESOME TALK, the other contestants who knew her immediately thought, "This is the one to beat."

A powerful and engaging speaker, she knew how to delight listeners on her radio program. Many thought she would be a natural. She also believed her radio skill would easily translate on stage.

She actually had to work harder.

A radio booth is a controlled environment. The host usually sits in a chair with a headset and a microphone. In the next room is the producer and/or audio tech who can be seen through a glass window and can give the host verbal cues. Guests can either be live with the host in the studio or plugged in remotely via the phone or other means.

The audience of a radio program is not seen. They listen in their homes, cars, or workplace. They are also separated from one another. They are not part of a large mass of people in one place, like a crowd in an auditorium. Their feedback typically is not immediate, except for radio call-in programs during which hosts engage with their guests directly.

The typical radio communication flow is linear—the sender (radio host) gives a message (content in the program) to the audience (listeners on the other end). The feedback is slow, screened, and is used to enhance whatever message the radio host is trying communicate. For example, if a listener calls into the radio program, the producer screens him or her in advance. If the producer agrees that the caller is appropriate to the situation, then that listener is patched into the broadcast. If not, that listener does not become part of the program.

The environment of a radio program is controlled.

The radio host shone when it came to conveying information. She knew how to articulate her ideas well, had a friendly demeanor, and spoke clearly. However, she did not know how to connect with an audience outside of a radio setting. Her skills as a radio host initially made her stiff.

She had to rewire herself to the environment and audience in a different way.

The content, environment, medium and purpose for the live speakers at the AWESOME TALK were different from those the radio host was accustomed to. When you are on stage giving a talk, you are not the host of a controlled program.

She had to loosen up, learn how to speak to the audience in a different way, and mitigate her "radio announcer voice." We all have this voice. It's that certain pitch and tone we *put on* when we are speaking in front of others.

She was challenged to guide an entirely different communication experience. As a radio host she was used to speaking *at* her audience. Now she had to speak *with* them in a different way. She also had to be more personable, self-revealing, and share stories. This is a similar struggle faced by the Instagram influencer we discussed a few chapters ago.

In the end, the radio host shifted her approach. She rewired her skills to fit the environment, context, and audience. She was certain and direct—skills she already possessed. But, she had to challenge herself to stop playing the role of radio host and, instead, focused on being a person with a heartfelt story. This was not an easy task, but one she faced head-on. She opened herself up and the audience embraced it with great respect.

Being a good speaker is not about being the perfect presenter. In fact, trying to be perfect often creates distance between you and your audience because you are not grounded in that moment. You are not wired.

Allow yourself to be flawed and real, and the audience will love you.

What's Right for that Moment?

Contextual communication is vital. There is no one-size-fits-all approach when it comes to public speaking. The way you are best able to express an idea and create impact with one audience may be different from the way you connect with another. Also, the medium in which you express that idea plays a part, as we saw with the radio announcer.

For example, you might take a different approach in your communication with a client than you do when you speak to an employee. The audience and relationship to each person is different and, therefore, you connect with them differently. Similarly, you might speak differently on the phone than you do when you are pitching a presentation live in the room to that same client.

The context, environment, medium, and purpose are different in both of those situations. On the phone, you are using a medium designed to give you some flexibility, and most likely its purpose is to review details and/or share some thoughts. When you do a pitch presentation, you are in a more controlled environment and the purpose is to make a sale. In each situation, you are wired differently.

A.W.E.S.O.M.E.

Being wired helps you to communicate well in that specific circumstance. It is based on a connection to the audience and the elements that may impact your ability to reach that individual or group of individuals. As the radio host demonstrated, these elements in her work environment include:

- Context—She hosts a program with a predetermined topic or idea.

- Environment—She is isolated in a room separated from the audience.

- Mediums—It is audio only; there is no visual support.

- Purpose—She is there to entertain and/or inform the audience.

Awaken Your Senses

Being wired also means awakening your senses to the context, environment, medium, and purpose. You get centered and realize your place in the overall experience. When you "show up," you are guiding this experience. It's important to do what you can to take it all in and activate yourself in a way to be fully present.

Jessica Weiner, a motivational speaker-turned-TV host, social and political activist, media personality, and branding expert, says this is what works for her:

Wired

It's important to me to feel fully present when I'm speaking in front of others. I need to know that I'm in my body and aware of my surroundings. So, when I'm about to step on stage or deliver an important presentation to a client, I take a moment to ground myself. I focus on the five senses:

1. What do I see? (I focus on what is right before me, whether a curtain, a person, or a wall)

2. What do I hear? (I focus on sounds of the room, my own breathing)

3. What do I feel? (I focus on the softness of my clothing or something I can hold)

4. What do I taste? (I pop a breath mint!)

5. What do I smell? (Hopefully something good! Food, coffee?)

The reason I do this is so that I am grounded in my physical reality and I'm able to get into my body. Then I'm in a more powerful position to speak and reach an audience.

What can you do to become alive in a public speaking situation? Are your senses alive? Are you wired?

A.W.E.S.O.M.E.

It's Electric!

In an electrical circuit panel in your home, the wires are connected to different rooms, and the voltage sent to each room is different. The voltage sent is appropriate for the estimated or maximum use in that room.

For example, a kitchen, which has major appliances like a refrigerator and electric dishwasher, requires more voltage than a living room, which may have only lamps and a TV that are used periodically.

Similarly, when you go to pitch, speak, or give a toast, you take into consideration "the room" and what is required for your successful delivery. You also awaken your senses so you can get a better sense of the audience. This allows you to be grounded and wired to what's around you. Add the three guiding principles—you are creative, skillful, and instinctive—and you become a strong volt of electricity that can light up the space and shine like a bright burst of energy.

Lesson Learned

When you are aligned and wired, you become immersed in the communication experience. You express your thoughts in a way that takes into consideration the dynamic between the sender (you), the message (what you have to say), and the receiver (your audience). Focusing on what your audience wants allows you to connect in a personal, effective way.

It is about their need, not yours. It is about how you can provide them an irresistible offer that is of service to them.

Summary

- Know your audience, understand what they value, and then determine how to best communicate what you have to offer them.

- Audiences don't want perfection; they want a connection. Speak with them, not at them.

- There is no one-size-fits-all approach to public speaking. Consider the environment, the context, and purpose of your message. Get wired to the overall experience.

- Awaken your senses when you are called to speak or present an idea. What do you see, hear, feel, taste, and smell? This allows you to get grounded in your physical environment and in your body, so you can be a powerful medium of communication.

Exercise

It's time to reflect and examine your awareness of the public speaking experience. Take a moment to think about your last public speaking experience and dissect the following four elements:

- The context
- The environment
- Mediums at your disposal
- Purpose of the pitch, talk, toast, or exchange

When you were called to speak, how aware were you of these elements? Looking back, what would you have done differently to be more wired to the situation? Would it have made a difference in your presentation?

Call to Action

Public speaking is a journey you create for your audience. Take time to consider what they want, the context, and physical environment before you speak.

Practice the mantra: *"I am connected to my higher purpose and wired to my surroundings. I am a gift."*

CHAPTER 8

Empathetic

Public speaking is a shared experience with the audience. They are you. You are one of them.

When you're *aligned,* you are connected to your expressive being. When you are *wired,* you are connected to your environment. When you are *empathetic,* you are connected to your audience.

These three elements overlap in certain ways. For example, being aligned and wired both include audience awareness. These three elements also work in unison to create a sense of A.W.E.

A sense of A.W.E. is that bright burning light within you that others experience. It is captivating. It is the shining unique you, the everyday celebrity, that draws people to you. It is internal power that, when harnessed, allows you to be seen and heard in a special way.

A spirit of A.W.E. is essential for public speaking.

Shared Experiences

Your audience is made up of real people and your understanding of the human experience allows you to connect with them. They are you; you are one of them. Speak with them in their totality—to their minds, hearts, and guts.

Witness your audience as they truly are, as individuals with feelings, thoughts, and values.

A.W.E.S.O.M.E.

Understand your audience—and become one of them. Choose to be inclusive. Relate to them because you have been where they've been and have experienced what they've experienced. Likewise, open up and allow listeners to see themselves in you.

On some level, you have a shared experience. This only comes about when you are honest with yourself and speak from the heart. When you are aligned and wired, you know how and when to use heartfelt stories—whether they are deeply sad, highly emotional, totally scary, or incredibly frustrating.

We are all flawed in some way. You might not like the pitch of your voice, the look of your hair, the rhythm in which you speak, but those imperfections connect you to an audience. While the audience may not have the same concerns, they may have an issue that creates a similar feeling. They can relate.

Relatability builds trust. Empathy builds connection. Both build better bonds between a speaker and the audience.

As a public speaker, make an effort to relate to others. You bring more than your expertise to the audience. You bring value. Too often we focus only on our talking points, but we have so much more to offer.

You are more accomplished and experienced than you choose to admit.

Empathetic

In the entertainment business, we're constantly selling ourselves to an audience. That audience might be moviegoers, a TV executive for a show we're pitching, or a casting agent for a project. We question whether they will value my movie, my project, or me. In this constant selling-yourself environment, it's sometimes hard to see your value clearly.

Michael Medico, a successful actor and TV director who spends much time in front of the camera and behind it, challenges the way we look at ourselves, regardless of the industry.

Often we don't know what we have to offer. We can't see our good traits. Even when people expound to us about our wonderful qualities, we can't hear them due to our low self-esteem, humbleness, or societal politeness.

Other times we see ourselves as a mix of what we haven't accomplished yet, and what we failed to do in the past. As soon as we conquer one thing on our super-goal list, it is gone. Then it's on to the next thing. We are always striving to accomplish more, to do the next big thing so often, we don't celebrate our accomplishments. Many times we don't even remember them, big or small.

Therefore, I find it helpful to list my accomplishments. All of them. From buying a home, to taking care of a parent, to writing a book or an article, to helping a neighbor, or getting that job offer. Gratitude for what you have accomplished really grounds us.

Indeed, gratitude is a useful tool. It gives you insight into your own internal strengths, how you might inspire others, and what others find attractive about you. Not only do your struggles allow you to empathize with others, so do your successes and accomplishments.

When you rise, you allow others to rise with you. They can see themselves in you. When it comes to empathy and public speaking, it is a two-way street. You, however, are the guiding force who sets the tone and potential for an empathetic exchange.

Passion, success, and accomplishments are great ways to draw in an audience. If you are sincere and honest, the audience will relate to you because they too have passion and accomplishments. It is our shining light, as well as our darkest nights—our human experiences in both—that others can relate to. The key is to be sincere. If you're not, you might lose an audience. Speaker and media personality, Julie Carrier, believes:

> Whatever you're feeling, your audience actually feels. So, if someone is up there giving a story that they *think* they should be saying, that they find to be personally boring, or not interesting—guess what? Your audience is going to think it's boring and not interesting.

But if you're sharing a story that is about what you care about, what you're passionate about, something that you care deeply about, you know what? Even if your audience before didn't really care about that subject or wasn't interested in that subject, they're going to catch that enthusiasm, and guess what? They're going to think you're an amazing speaker because you're operating from a place of authenticity, passion, excitement, and emotion.

Authentic passion is contagious. It is like a magnet that pulls people into your sphere of excitement. Others are eager to feel your enthusiasm. They identify with your emotion, even if they may not have initially liked the subject. They relate and are empathetic to the experience. They feel connected.

Let's look at an example of an audience's connection to a speaker from the AWESOME TALK.

The Restaurateur

Emily and I were immediately wowed by the restaurateur's audition video. Right from the beginning, he shared his passion for poker. In fact, in the video, he was sitting behind a poker table with cards in his hands, and used these props masterfully as he spoke.

His dream was to open a restaurant casino. While neither

A.W.E.S.O.M.E.

Emily nor I are big card players, we were attracted to his enthusiasm. He not only spoke about his ambition, he embodied it. You could see, hear, and feel his conviction.

As we worked with him on his AWESOME TALK, we wanted to know more about his passion. He got us immediately interested, but now that he had our attention, what was next? What was his plan? Did he merely want us to know his passion or was there more?

A confident, good-looking, and charming man, people were naturally drawn to this restaurateur. As with other attractive people, he now had to do something with this attention. What was it?

What was he going to give his audience? Was he going to stimulate them? Inspire them? Transform them? What was the journey only he could lead them on?

This is a question all speakers must address ahead of time: what's the impact I am going to make?

The restaurateur shared a story from his childhood. He recalled where he first got his passion for success. He took the audience on a journey—from being a young boy influenced by his father, to being a dad himself who wants to make a difference in this world.

In his talk he spoke about personal struggles he faced in pursuing his dream of opening a restaurant casino. It didn't matter what the struggle was; it only mattered that the audience related to it—the emotion, the trials, and the success.

He showed exactly what a speaker is capable of and needs to do. Once the audience is listening, deliver. You've been handed the microphone; say something. Once the audience is looking at you, express yourself. The spotlight has found you. It's time to share your passion, your greatest purpose.

Keep up the momentum.

Rick Tamlyn, media personality, speaker, and author of *Play Your Bigger Game*, works with people on creating impact and he says:

> It sounds so simplistic, but it's profound when people get it. They're no longer anxious about performing. They're in transmitter mode. They're in impact mode— they want to impact.

The restaurateur lured in the audience with a personal story and ultimately motivated them with a simple, yet powerful, message: "I can do it. You can do it. We can do it."

He chose to be a medium that inspired others. He transmitted his message and made a huge impact.

A.W.E.S.O.M.E.

S.I.T.

Before you speak, ask yourself:

- What kind of medium (of communication) am I going to be?
- What's the impact I am going to make?

Like the restaurateur, are you going to share a story of struggle and triumph? Like the rock star, will you showcase a creative talent? Like the socialite, are you willing to be vulnerable?

Each of these speakers, although in front of different audiences with different kinds of presentations, decided ahead of time the impact they wanted to make. They considered what they were going to give their audience and the journey they were going to guide them on.

As I often point out in my coaching work, seducing audiences begins before you even open your mouth. Decide ahead of time what your agenda and call to action will be. Sound familiar? This is **The A Factor**, as described in my book, *Everyday Celebrity*. The A Factor is:

- Know your **A**udience
- Determine your **A**genda
- Create a call to **A**ction

Empathetic

Once the A Factor is determined, there is another step to take in order to be well prepared for any speaking engagement. Decide *how* you are going to connect with your audience by knowing the purpose of your message. You need to **S.I.T.** before you speak.

S.I.T. is an acronym that stands for **S**timulate, **I**nspire and **T**ransform. Deciding ahead of time whether you are going to stimulate, inspire, or transform your audience will help you find ways to relate and connect to them. Use this goal to prepare your talk. It will help determine what stories to include, what emotions to share, and how to harness your empathy.

Here's a breakdown of **S.I.T.**:

- **St**imulate: Stir up your audience. Get them to think.
- **I**nspire: Lift up their spirits. Enlighten them. Educate them.
- **T**ransform: Get them to take action.

Let's use the example of speaking to employees at a company meeting. How might you S.I.T. before you speak to them?

- If you intend to stimulate them, you would prepare stats and figures from where the company was a year ago to where it is today.

A.W.E.S.O.M.E.

- If you are going to inspire them, you might also include a personal success story of your own, a time when you were behind on your goals and how someone motivated you to get ahead.

- If you want to transform them, then you might also include new targets and offer incentives.

Depending on the goal—whether it's to stimulate, inspire, or transform—different layers or talking points may be added to the presentation. Consider what stories, examples, and personal revelations are going to work best with your intention. What will you say that relates to them? Are you engaged in a way that is personal and connected to them? Are you empathetic and direct?

Empathy in action is powerful, as TV programming executive and on-air pop culture expert, Brian Balthazar, points out:

> When someone is relatable it feels like they're sharing something with you, whereas, if they're not relatable, they're just telling you something. For any speaking engagement, you really want to strive for that human connection: here's what we have in common and here's why the information I've learned you can learn from, because we are more alike than we are different.

> If someone is not relatable, you feel isolated from him or her. You're not even sure if their information is

going to be useful to you. But if you feel like, "Wow, this person and I have something in common, and they are sharing a mistake, something they learned the hard way, or something they learned in the course of their life," it can help you avoid the same problem or avoid the same mistake. That's an incredibly valuable discussion.

A.W.E.S.O.M.E.

Lesson Learned

Empathy works two ways: first, it is the connection you have to your audience's feelings, experiences, and values. Second, it is how they relate to your accomplishments, trials, and passion. Be bold enough to share the best of yourself, acknowledging both, your successes and lessons learned through your struggles. Be the gift the audience wants and needs.

Summary

- Be personal and self-revealing with your audience. Let them know you've been where they've been and you've experienced what they've experienced.

- Passion is a magnet and your enthusiasm about it is attractive. Others are eager to experience your excitement, so allow that emotion to fuel your message.

- Set your intention with an audience. Decide beforehand if you want to Stimulate, Inspire, or Transform them. **S.I.T.** (*the acronym for stimulate, inspire, or transform*) before you speak.

- Once you know your intention, use it to determine what stories, examples, and personal revelations are best going to accomplish the goal of reaching your audience the best way possible.

Exercise

This is a moment when it's all about you! Make a list of your personal accomplishments. Try to think of as many as possible, and make sure it is no less than ten. Next to each accomplishment mark an S for stimulate, I for inspire, and T for transform. Keep adding to this list, whether it is something that you remember or a new success that you achieve. This is your go-to list for future public speaking opportunities.

Call to Action

Connect to your audience and allow them to connect to you by being relatable, self-revealing, and empathetic.

Practice the mantra: *"I open myself up so that my story may stimulate, inspire, and transform others."*

QUOTABLE MENTIONS ABOUT BEING IN A.W.E.

The following are more thoughts and advice about being aligned, wired, and empathetic. What entertainment professionals say about being…

ALIGNED

"It's really refreshing when you're talking to someone and they have no idea just how special they are… and you can see it."
– Tim Curtis,
  Talent Agent

"I think you can tell when someone is sitting there, and just dripping in who they are."
– Mishawn Nolan,
  Entertainment Attorney

"I always try to speak from my heart, my gut. I don't try to be clever. That doesn't mean I don't add humor. Humor is in my gut. But I don't try to sound smart or clever."
– Michael Medico,
  Actor and TV Director

WIRED

"Smile. Smiling gives off so much energy. It gives off, like, 'Oh, wow, I really want to get to know that person.'"
– Jill Bandemer,
  Reality TV Casting
  Producer

"Think about what even the shyest person is capable of doing under extraordinary circumstances. When we must act, we do."
– Andi Matheny,
  Acting Coach

"Much of life is pretty ridiculous, and what is getting the most attention is not often the most important thing, so being able to laugh at that is so important."
– Brian Balthazar,
  TV Executive and
  Media Personality

EMPATHETIC

"I think my best advice is to be respectful of what you're endeavoring to do, but to not take it too seriously. And find a way to have fun with it, or to at least enjoy it."
– Ric Enriquez,
  Casting Director
  and Producer

"Speaking, or putting yourself out there, is one of the most vulnerable things you can do. You're basically saying, 'Look at me, I have something important to say.'"
– Zachary Bilemdjian,
  Costumer and Stylist

"I find people that are charismatic are very empathetic. They're really great at emanating something that says that they relate to everyone."
– Sharon Hashimoto,
  Editor and Director

CHAPTER 9
Simple

You are the best medium of communication.

When you are connected to yourself, your environment, and your audience, you are in A.W.E. The overwhelming feeling of admiration and connection the audience has with you—and that you have with the audience—shows you are aligned, wired, and empathetic. You become the best medium of communication for your message.

The next four steps for being A.W.E.S.O.M.E. give life to that feeling of A.W.E. Your pitch, speech, toast, or video is an experience. It is no longer just an idea or thought. It has a life of its own.

Why is It All So Complicated?

We get into our heads when the stakes to deliver a message are high. For example, when we really want a job or to make the sale, we give extra weight to the message and experience. If we don't do it "right" we literally might lose money, but if we do it "right" we have gained so much more.

Not only do we get money, but our self-esteem also gets a boost. It's a win-win situation. The person on the other end gets a quality product (whether it's our service or an actual physical item), and we are validated personally and financially.

On the surface, it is a pretty straightforward exchange: "I have something you want. Do you want it?"

Yet we add so much more to this situation. We attach meaning of our personal worth—the idea of whether or not we are, indeed, "good enough."

In the example of my high school election speech, I wanted to prove that I was not only good enough, but better than my opponent. I wanted the position of student body treasurer so badly that I tried a gimmick. The truth is, the "it" I wanted was approval and acceptance.

It gets more complicated than necessary, and this is not limited to sales dialogues or high school election speeches. It happens often and in many different situations. For example, when one gives a keynote address or speaks on video, the presenter may get so caught up in the medium that it becomes overwhelming. He or she may obsess about the number of eyes or ears that are paying attention.

I can't tell you the number of times a would-be speaker, like the socialite, broke down in tears just over the idea of being on a stage. Or how many times I've had to calm the fears of experts who wanted to shoot a YouTube video. The thought of being on camera brings up many insecurities.

This leads us back to the struggle between trying to be fearless and the potential of what being **fearFULL** can do for us in public speaking. Fear is fuel that can turn nervousness into excitement. How we look at the situation is paramount.

Simple

Our minds can create something that is much bigger than it needs to be. In the end, and as we've already stated, there is a basic communication cycle (Diagram 6B) in which there is a sender (you), a message (your presentation), a receiver (the audience), and feedback (their attention). Worry and anxiety are a form of static, an interference that impacts the experience even before we open our mouths.

You can unnecessarily complicate a talk when you rely solely on things outside of yourself to make a point. This occurs when you believe that you are not enough. Even though you might believe in your content, you may not believe in your ability to deliver it. You don't fully grasp that you are the message.

When you begin to stress out and complicate the situation, just stop. Remember your fear can be fuel for your presentation. And when I say fuel, think of it in simple terms, like a good breakfast that starts out the day.

The entertainment business is not just a creative enterprise; it's a business that involves meetings, negotiations, and presentations. Talent agent Tim Curtis notes when using tools, props, and gadgets can go wrong:

> There's nothing worse for me than when we're going to a presentation and there are projections or slides and someone sits there and reads me the slide verbatim. It's one thing to sort of put an idea up on the

screen and say, this is a talking point, a thinking point, a quote, or something like that, but I don't need you to read me your presentation because I do know how to read and I'll probably read it a lot faster than you're able to articulate it.

The other thing is giving handouts to people at meetings, because once you've given someone a handout, you've lost them. All they're going to be doing is sitting there, reading through what you've given them, flipping through the pages. They're not going to be listening to what you're telling them, and that's so much more valuable than what is on the page.

If you want to give them a handout, give it to them at the end of the meeting so they have something to take with them.

Speakers sometimes wander off point. Not only does this happen in meetings, but also online and in videos. Editor and director, Sharon Hashimoto, sets forth the importance of simplicity:

I think it's very important to be very concise about what you say. People tune out very easily nowadays. I think simplicity leaves the most impact with people.

Bullet points are really easy to take home, usually if you give people three to five bullet points, they'll remember at least one or two... especially if they're useful points.

Simple

Let's look at an example of someone who embodied this idea of simplicity.

The Financial Advisor

The financial advisor had all he needed when he showed up to the AWESOME TALK. He had a warm and charming disposition, so it was no surprise that he received the award as "the most popular speaker."

His friendly personality radiated the moment he walked on stage. Once people saw his smile and the gleam in his eyes, they were assured that this was someone worth their attention. He made the audience feel comfortable and relaxed.

As we prepared for the AWESOME TALK, Emily and I asked what props he might use. Was he interested in using a video or images in a PowerPoint?

Surprisingly, he didn't want to use any elements. Others we had worked with used too many elements in their talks, like a thirty-slide presentation. Pleased, but cautious, we encouraged him to make sure he didn't need any visual support. He agreed to think about it some more.

Due to a work commitment, he missed the coaching session where speakers practiced their presentations. We asked him to practice his talk in front of a friend or two to help clarify whether or not visuals would enhance his talk.

A.W.E.S.O.M.E.

The financial advisor took what we said to heart. He practiced on his own and came up with three slides that he wanted to use during his presentation. This was the least amount used by any of the AWESOME TALK speakers.

We asked the financial advisor during the next rehearsal why only so few. He commented, "Because that was all that's needed."

He was right!

His talk focused on his volunteer trip to help rebuild Haiti after a 7.0 earthquake devastated many towns and villages. He observed firsthand how locals mobilized together with volunteers to turn tragedy into a triumph of the human spirit. The people of Haiti did not let this crisis destroy their positive nature. Instead, they showed gratitude and graciousness with each other and every person who came to help them.

His experience in Haiti had a profound effect on him and was the foundation for the theme of his talk: how to overcome adversity, no matter what the setback or struggle. He articulated this theme eloquently and his three visuals supported it in a simple, yet impactful fashion.

The first slide showed Haiti before the earthquake. The second showed the devastation. The third showed the people with volunteers, smiling together as they rebuilt their homes.

Simple

These three moments captured in photographs were powerful in their simplicity.

The financial advisor's volunteer work not only touched him on a personal level, it also challenged his professional outlook. He saw his customers differently. Financial adversity had crippled some of his clients. He wanted to be of service to them on a deeper level, and help them overcome their fears, setbacks or struggles. He wanted them to find hope again.

The profound lesson we learned from the financial advisor was to take time to flesh out your presentation, fine-tune it, and keep it simple. Had he showed more images, he would have risked his talk becoming only about himself as a volunteer. Those additional images would have distracted from his end goal – how to face challenges head-on and thrive.

In the end, he gave the audience some insight into his private world. He used the volunteer experience as an example of how being of service to his clients really means looking at their lives and needs, no matter the situation. He used charming storytelling and emotion to embody the message.

Anything more would have complicated the communication exchange. He kept it simple, and used exactly what served his story.

A.W.E.S.O.M.E.

What's Really Needed?

When a speaker gives "all that's needed" for a talk, he or she truly shines. Why? The focus of the message is the shared experience, not the potentially over-complicated elements. How do you know what's just right? Test it.

When you prepare for a presentation or talk, keep these very simple ideas in mind:

1. What is the topic of my talk?

2. What's the goal of my presentation?
   Is it to stimulate, inspire, or transform? S.I.T.

3. Define your talking points; limit them to five.

4. Create a list of potential elements that might enhance your presentation, pitch or video.
   These can include props, visuals, or music.

5. Outline your presentation.
   (See potential formats below.)

6. Practice it twice.
   Practice it twice in front of the same person, once with the elements and a second time without.

Once you get to the practice, ask your volunteer listener, "Did I achieve the goal of my talk? Were my talking points clear and the elements necessary?" Once you get the volunteer's feedback, you can make adjustments.

As for potential formats, here are a few that might help.

Simple

The 5-Paragraph Essay

This is a writing tool that many of us in the US learned when we were in grade school. You start with a thesis, give three supporting facts or assertions, and then offer a conclusion. For example:

1. California is a great place for me to live.

2. It's sunny.

3. The entertainment business is based here.

4. This is where I was raised and my family lives here.

5. While I've lived in other places, this seems perfect for me because it's where I work, enjoy the outdoors, and spend time with my family. I invite you to experience this wonderful place.

One important item to add to your conclusion is a **call to action**. It adds depth and excitement. In the example above, the call to action was the invitation to experience "my California."

The Inverted Pyramid

This is one of the writing styles taught in journalism classes. In this model, you start with the main headline or newsworthy item and then offer other details about the main headline. For example:

A.W.E.S.O.M.E.

- Jess Ponce III travels to Asia on December 15 for the release of his new book with Emily Liu.

  - The book will be available in bookstores this week.

  - They will be doing two events, one on December 17 and another on December 19.

  - The book will be available in English and Chinese.

  - This is their second book.

  - Buy your copy of their new book today and join them at one of their upcoming events.

Again, in this model, I encourage you to create a call to action. Get your audience to do something. Be direct and clear, so there is no confusion.

Flashback/Flash-forward

This is a great model for storytelling that adds a touch of drama. The three points are (1) what happened, (2) what you did, and (3) where you are now. For example:

1. Sally had a bad car accident that changed her life.
2. A drunk driver hit her sedan and she was hospitalized for a week.
3. She now provides counseling to drunk drivers and

their families. She has turned a personal tragedy into service for others. If she can do that, what can you do in your life?

As with the first two, this last example also includes a call to action. This is an important and an impactful tool that is essential for public speaking. It underscores why you are speaking to this audience and helps you achieve your goal, whether that is to stimulate, inspire, or transform (S.I.T.) your audience.

These tools are all intended to help you reach your audience in a simple, direct way. And remember, don't be in your head too much. It's important to speak from your heart, by using all of your facial expressions. Your smile, face and eyes convey emotion, a wide range of feelings from joy to sadness.

A popular saying is the "eyes are the windows to the soul." I also believe that our eyes are an invitation to a journey — a heart's journey. Be bold. Invite others on this journey with you.

The best and most powerful medium of expression is you. This is where being in A.W.E. (aligned, wired, and empathetic) becomes your greatest barometer as to whether or not a tool or other external device is needed.

When in doubt, keep it simple.

Lesson Learned

Get out of your own way. Focusing solely on the outcome or situation (such as being on stage in front of hundreds of people or doing a video that lives online forever) can make you crazy. Minimize your anxiety and self-doubt by focusing only on what's necessary to make your point. What essential points are needed to create the impact you want? Allow the topic and intention of your talk to guide you in developing your talking points, format, and flow.

Summary

- Get out of your head. Be in the moment to avoid making your pitch, talk, or toast more complicated than necessary.

- Don't be overwhelmed or intimidated with technique. If you don't need it, don't use it. That includes PowerPoints, handouts, props, and other elements you might use in your talk.

- When a speaker gives "all that's needed" for a talk, he or she truly shines. Follow this process:

  1. What is the topic of my talk?

  2. What's the goal of my talk?

  3. Define your talking points; limit them to five.

4. Create a list of potential elements that might enhance your talk.

5. Outline your presentation.

6. Practice it twice.

- Keep your format easy and direct. Here are three potentials to consider:
  - The 5-Paragraph Essay
  - The Inverted Pyramid
  - Flashback/Flash-forward

Exercise

It's now time to practice. Go into your pantry, cupboard, or junk drawer right now and grab two items. Pick the first two you see.

Next, prepare two different ninety-second presentations. Identify which of the sample formats you want to use for item #1: The 5-Paragraph Essay, The Inverted Pyramid or Flashback/Flash-forward. Then pick another format or one that you create for item #2.

Use the six-step preparation model, above, for each talk.

After you've given your presentation, reflect on a few things. What format did you like? How did following the six-step preparation model help—or not help—you get ready for this presentation? What could you have done differently? What did you learn about your own inclinations to make the presentation complicated or easy?

Call to Action

Simplicity and complication are both a state of mind. Choose wisely.

Practice the mantra: *"I am the most powerful medium of communication."*

CHAPTER 10

Open

*Be in the moment and embrace the unknown.
What you experience might just change you
and those you're speaking to.*

Countless books and authors tell you "to be in the moment," but what does that really mean? It is a call to action: allow yourself to be part of the experience.

When you are connected to your audience, you instinctively know what to do to convey your message. If you doubt what you should do, it's probably not right. Listen to your intuition.

The Road is Still Unknown

Even though you have a roadmap for your speech, the experience takes on a life of its own. Some elements are unpredictable and uncontrollable, such as the mood of the room, potential outside noise like a lawnmower, distracted audience members, and countless others. You may also make natural mishaps of your own doing, such as getting lost in a phrase or forgetting a point.

These disruptions are part of the overall experience, and you can be much more effective by integrating them into your message. Ignoring them or trying to over-compensate for these "mistakes" rarely ever works. Pause for a second and take the next best course of action.

Comedians do this masterfully. World-renowned actor and comedian, Angelo Tsarouchas, describes this as "the save":

A.W.E.S.O.M.E.

If I do something wrong, there's a split-second decision to go for the save, or divert it to a different segue.

I was in a club in Chicago, The Improv. When you get on stage, it's dark. You've got really bright lights on you, and you can faintly see the front row. I saw this guy in a jacket, wearing sunglasses with a hat, and I'm like "Who is this guy?"

I did a couple of jokes and said, "Look at this guy—too cool for school. Dude, what's with the sunglasses? What, are you too cool for the room? Are you in the wrong club—is it a jazz club? Or what do you think, you're Ray Charles? What's going on here?"

Nobody laughed. Then one woman said, "Sir, he's got a guide dog. He's blind."

I breathed. I let it settle in and, without really apologizing, I said, "Sir, I didn't see your dog." I felt like the biggest asshole in the world. The man in the front row said, "Son, just go on, you're really funny. Don't worry about me." He was cool about it.

I had to turn it around. I put it back on me and said, "Wait, I was the one trying to be cool and clever. Look what happened. This shit blew up in my face." And the crowd appreciated the fact that I owned it.

Open

I said hello to the guy after my set. He said, "I know you didn't see my guide dog because you went on, because the way you were talking to me I realized you didn't know yet. But that's ok, 'cause it was funny."

If you ever watch *Jeopardy*, even the experts make mistakes. Alex Trebek will come back going, "Well, actually, Dave was right. The answer was you know, the Azores, it wasn't the Galapagos Islands." They give it back. I think it humanizes you to an audience, or to whomever you're speaking to, and it also shows them that you're just like them. We can all make mistakes."

Comedians know how to be open because they have to— every time they're on stage something can happen. They often incorporate the unpredictable experiences into their act. They are in the moment and connected to the experience. They prepare for the unexpected.

You too can integrate uncontrollable elements when you're navigating a speaking experience. It's a matter of how you choose to look at the situation. Are you there to control the message or guide it? Do you seek perfection or embrace imperfect reality as an asset? What do you value most: you, the audience, your shared experience, or all three?

Your approach to the unknown is important. Your reaction to it is vital. Being open allows both the known and un-known to be a part of the experience. Being closed gives the elements outside of your control unlimited power.

A.W.E.S.O.M.E.

When you focus on controlling every element of the environment, you actually weaken your ability to be effective. The temptation to pay special attention to moments that go wrong, or even right, can distract you from your greater purpose when you are speaking—and that is to be the message. Let everything around you—the good and bad—fuel you, not distract you. Be open to the experience.

Here's an example of a speaker who opened herself to the speaking journey.

The Dancer

The dancer came to the AWESOME TALK with earnest sincerity. She was intense and full of emotion. Emily and I could see it in her eyes and hear it in her words, but we didn't witness this passion in her being.

Even though her eyes gleamed and she spoke with conviction, she didn't embody the message. For someone who used her body as an expressive tool in dance, she wasn't using this tool in her talk. She held back. Something was missing.

We challenged her to do a small dance in her presentation. I remember when we first asked her to do this. She looked at us as if to say, "Really? You want me to dance?"

Open

"Yes, we do."

Even though she was a little reluctant, she agreed to do it. At first it was awkward because she didn't believe dancing and talking were connected. However, one thing was very apparent; when she danced, she had an expressive quality that was missing when she spoke. When she incorporated her dance with her words, she soared. Her message was heard with her purposeful intent.

When you take a step back, it's not hard to see the connection between dancing and speaking because both of them are about expressing yourself. In a talk, you reveal an idea and emotion. In dancing, it's similar.

Dancing increased her range as a speaker. She could be serious and understated in one moment (when she spoke), then lively and grand in the next (when she moved). She just had to open herself up to actually doing a dance on stage, but as part of a talk, not as a dance performance alone. This terrified her.

We asked her to literally speak, dance, and then speak again. Figuratively, this is part of what all speakers are called to do. As a speaker, you express thoughts, take in the environment, dance with your audience, and speak some more.

Like the dancer, a speaker is also called to use his or her most poignant tools. For some of us, like comedian Angelo

Tsarouchas, it might be comedy. For others, it might be storytelling. Whatever it is, each of us has a strong communication asset that, when expressed purposefully, can make us great speakers.

Passion and Joy

What is your communication asset? How do you know you're tapping into your own special way of expressing yourself, such as comedy or dancing?

Andi Matheny, professional actor, host, and founder of Andi Matheny Acting Studios, believes it starts with passion.

> One universal truth I've found is everyone feels passionately about something. It may be politics, religion, or the merits of baking with real butter, but everyone has a passionate belief. One of the first exercises in my class, which is explained in more detail in my book, is for my actors to talk about their passion. Some can delve into it easily. I can talk passionately— completely unrehearsed—about at least a dozen topics, from animal rights to the merits of Peanut M&M's. The most important thing is: *It doesn't matter what it is.* All that matters is you feel passionately about it.
>
> After this exercise, I ask the actor where in their body

they felt a physical connection. They usually point to either their heart or their solar plexus area—the area of strong connection.

Here's an exercise Andi does in her acting class to see where passion lives.

Think of something you feel passionately about. Walk around your room. Start to rant [about your passion]. Get it all out. Notice how you not only feel great, you'll also feel that gut connection. That's your passion that you've just effortlessly connected to, and it will be in your muscle memory going forward.

This exercise is crucial for actors. Actors must know what they feel passionate about because dramas—and comedies—are often written about a character who feels passionately about something. They must understand and have empathy for their character's passion, or else the portrayal will be an empty shell, hackneyed. And you can't fool us—if you're not feeling it, we're not feeling it either.

So what if you're not an actor? Whether you're a salesman, a teacher, a public speaker, or a politician, you must also have access to your passion. If you're giving a speech or a sales pitch but you're not connected to the material—it's going to feel like pushing a boulder up Mt. Everest.

A.W.E.S.O.M.E.

But if you feel that passionate connection—your speech will take wings.

And why is joy so important? I believe it is one of the most fundamental modes of expression, but we often forget it because of self-induced pressure. Andi has this to say about joy:

> When I was a child, the event of self-expression gave me joy, or great delight and happiness because I didn't want anything from it other than the *joy of the event itself.*

> More plainly—I didn't want approval. I didn't want a job. I didn't want to get hired on a TV show. I didn't want a casting director to like me. I wasn't performing in order to get *something* or some *outcome.* I simply wanted to feel the joy of the moment, of expressing myself, and of sharing something I was passionate about. So it turns out, when we're children, we're a lot smarter than we think.

Joy and passion are wonderful barometers to gauge when you're in the moment, connected to your audience, and wired to the experience. Focus on your passion, not the quest for approval, or the desired outcome of your talk, such as a job or money. Those results happen because the audience experiences your passion and believes in you.

Open

Talent Agent Tim Curtis describes this moment when he receives pitches:

> If they believe it, I'm much more likely to believe it. If there's doubt or hesitation on their side, then I'm probably going to be immediately turned off. If they're not making eye contact, if they're hesitating in any way, if their facts aren't correct, if there's any sort of hole in the presentation that I can find, I probably will. Then it's just over. But if they come in fully prepared and genuinely engaged, supporting and believing what they're talking about, I'm far more likely to be impressed.

When the dancer's passion was clearly expressed in her dance movements, her joy was evident. With each graceful wave of her hand, thoughtful step, or longing gaze, she guided us. She embodied the message, believed in it, and made an impression on us.

Take a Beat

You, too, can create the same opportunity and impression with an audience if you tap into your passion and foster your most expressive gift. What can help you do this? Often it is being still and silent.

When Angelo decided to go for "the save" and own up to making a mistake with the blind man, he had to take a beat.

A.W.E.S.O.M.E.

He stopped, got connected to the environment, was one with his audience, and then spoke. He was not defensive.

How often do you do the same? Do you take a beat or get defensive? It's hard because nobody wants to make a mistake and it's embarrassing when it happens. However, when you keep on talking after a misstep, you risk making the situation worse.

Often, we repeat ourselves and keep on rambling in an unproductive fashion because we are uncomfortable. We don't like silence. Yet, even if it's just a moment to pause, collect ourselves, and then move forward, silence speaks volumes.

Silence can also draw people into you, help you redirect your talk, or make a point.

The dancer successfully used the power of silence. She stopped talking when she started to dance and this silence drew the audience even deeper into her story. Her multidimensional approach proved to be effective: speak, be silent, dance, and then speak again.

Silence is an especially powerful tool when you are speaking to a large audience. Quiet moments make people stop and pay attention. They listen even more intently after the pause.

Internal silence is also powerful. It can help you reconnect

Open

to the joy of your inner child and allow your passionate and expressive self to be heard over the ambient noise of self-doubt and nervousness. It helps you to be more open.

A.W.E.S.O.M.E.

Lesson Learned

Get comfortable with the idea that you might be in uncomfortable situations when you speak. Anything can happen—from mishaps and technical issues to environmental distractions to saying something "wrong." How you handle these situations can make or break your success as a public speaker. Pause, take a beat, and go for the save by redirecting the conversation. Remember you are orchestrating an experience for the audience.

Summary

- Potential disruptions may occur in public speaking, including unpredictable elements and natural mishaps of your own doing. How you react to them is critically important.

- You can integrate uncontrollable elements into your presentation if you are willing to let go of "perfection." Choose whether you will let distractions take you out of the moment—or if you will pivot and use them to your advantage.

- Passion is everything. If you believe in your subject, your audience will believe in it, too. Even the smallest doubt may turn them off.

- Get comfortable with silence. It is a powerful tool that draws in an audience. It also keeps you from rambling and repeating yourself, because you embrace the idea of taking a beat.

Exercise

Are you ready to be bold? Go to a local coffee shop, shopping mall, or other public place. Ask one or two random people to be your audience. Then do your presentation from the previous chapter.

Once you are finished, take note of potential disruptions that happened during your talk, such as the environment, other people, or ambient noise. Also, pay attention to your own internal disruptions, such as your anxiety, excitement, nervousness or other self-dialogue.

Then ask your audience two questions: (1) What did they think of your presentation? (2) How do they feel you handled the distractions?

Feel free to have a dialogue with them about the experience.

Call to Action

Let go of control and immerse yourself in the speaking experience. The unpredictable and unknown are gifts you can use as a speaker.

Practice the mantra: *"I embrace the unknown. It is a gift."*

CHAPTER 11

Magical

*That moment when you show up
exactly as you need to be.*

There is that moment when words show up exactly as you need them... when you are one with the audience. The experience takes on a life of its own. You are the message and the message is you. This is magic.

A Moment in Time

We create magic when we embrace every communication situation as its own unique experience. Like snowflakes, no two moments are exactly the same. While they may be similar, certain elements—such as the specific audience, the environment, or your delivery—make that moment in time, that connection, special and distinct.

You cannot repeat a moment; you can only create new ones. Therefore, be a magician, not a replicator.

Jess Weiner, media commentator, branding expert and self-described "actionist," says this about being magical:

In order to truly connect with people, we have to give the audience our true self on that stage and that can be a very vulnerable place. Yet that vulnerability leaves us open to those moments of unexpected magic when you say something that truly resonates or excites. Providing those game-changing thought-starters for people is what I aim for every time.

I think each individual has his or her own unique style

and presence that takes a while to develop and fine-tune. You'll never live into your power as a speaker if you are trying to copy "the greats." You have something to offer audiences that no one else can, because you have unique experiences that provide a point of view unlike any other. You have to lean into that.

You cannot teach passion and you cannot shortcut through the messy work of self-discovery. That sense of passion and a deep knowing of oneself leaves you open to create all kinds of magic in your life, both on stage and off.

I remember the moment I met Jess Weiner. My office was right next to a studio, and while I looked out the window over the soundstages, she walked in, a bundle of energy. She was also remarkably grounded and connected.

My boss introduced her, then turned to my colleagues and me and said, "She's it." I would soon discover exactly what she meant. One of Jess's greatest assets was that she intuitively knew something we've already discussed: that she herself is the most powerful medium possible. The format doesn't matter.

Whether on a live stage, a blog post, or a TV show, she understood her gift and how to communicate it. She was a conduit. And I had the pleasure of working with this motivational speaker and self-esteem expert over the next few months—and learned the magic of being a conduit that lit up every audience she engaged and every room she walked into.

Be a Conduit

When you lean into your expertise and passion, do what you love, and practice it regularly, you become a conduit. Others witness that something special only you have. They are drawn to your irresistible offer. It might be noticed as, "Wow, she's really confident" or "Look at his charisma."

What these comments and others like them are pointing to is your ability to communicate something greater than yourself. They don't see just you. They see your magic.

Magic appears in different ways. Sometimes it hits an audience like an impressive high note from a singer or grabs them like an exhilarating, heart-pounding scene from an action film. Sometimes magic is softer and touches an audience like a sweet, tender ballad in a romance movie or mesmerizes them like the first day of spring.

Everyone's magical potion is unique. What one speaker conjures up may not work for another. Here are questions to consider when identifying your own magic:

- Who needs or wants what I have?

- What can I say or do to best express my irresistible offer?

- Where are my mind, heart, and intuition when I begin to speak? Am I aligned?

- When am I most connected to the environment and audience? Am I wired and empathetic?

- Why is this important now, in this moment?

- How am I most impactful?

Examining "who you are" and "how you are" when you're called to deliver a message empowers you to be a better speaker. You can better align your expressive self, get wired to your environment, and create magical moments.

Here's a speaker who did just that.

The Stylist

He was a quiet person, but by no means was he shy. He had a subtle charm that made you feel warm and comfortable almost immediately. A definitive individual, he didn't hesitate to state an opinion or thought.

As a stylist, he practiced these skills with his clients. After all, when you deal with someone's appearance, such as a client's hairstyle or make up, you also address the client's insecurities. You are called to offer reassurance, guidance, and validation. These attributes seemed to be a natural part of his demeanor.

For the AWESOME TALK, he decided to share his coming-out story. He spoke about his journey of self-discovery and acceptance as a gay man. He took the audience on a deeply personal and vulnerable odyssey.

He expressed his struggles and triumphs with just the right amount of drama and emotion. He wasn't loud or "big," nor was he overly emotional or sappy. He took charge and delivered his message in a personal way, using his eyes and facial expressions.

He smiled, sometimes shyly looked away, and other times had a determined gleam in his eyes when he spoke. Whatever his expression, it was appropriate to that part of the story, and he remained connected to those listening to him throughout each beat. For example, when he spoke about his mentor, you could see both the sadness in his eyes, missing this deceased person now, as well as the joy he had in his heart having met this person.

He used his body as an expressive medium. When he made a serious point about a friend who could not accept he was gay, he stood tall, stiff, and showed little movement. In contrast, when he spoke about self-love, his body was relaxed, his movements were soft, and he seemed to shine from within.

A.W.E.S.O.M.E.

He had powerful presence. He was grounded and in the moment with his heart, mind, and gut in full alignment. Powerful presence is often misinterpreted as "forceful." This leads some speakers to be boisterous, commanding, or grandiose.

He showed up authentically and captivated the audience with his own unique speaking style. Yes, there were emotional tears, but they weren't for effect. They were real because they embodied the emotion and thoughts he was experiencing during each story point. It was as if the audience was there, feeling what he felt at certain moments.

When you're fully aligned, immersed in the communication experience, and the right words and actions just seem to show up, that's when you know you are in flow. Your instinct guides you in how to be the message in that moment. You become a conduit. You are an instrument of expression. You channel magic.

An Honest Connection

In the entertainment business, we are constantly on the hunt for this magical experience. Reality and game show casting producer, Jill Bandemer, describes seeing that magic in potential contestants:

It happens when you love everything they're saying.

Magical

You say to yourself, "I would love to sit and have a meal with this person." You just can't get enough. You get this great vibe, this great energy from that individual. I feel like those are the people that you want in your home when you're watching TV. You want to let those people into your life.

When your audience wants more of you, that's when you know that you've touched something personal in them. They are under a spell. Your magical being—the way your words, actions, and emotions flow—is attractive to that individual.

A personal connection is magical. As Jill describes it, people want to invite you into their homes (literally and figuratively). Something about you and what you are saying offers them something they want or need. It doesn't matter how similar the two of you are. In fact, you can be totally different from each other.

What matters is that you are authentically connected. It has to be real. *You* have to be real.

The stylist didn't focus on whether or not others could relate to his being gay. He focused on being true to his story and his emotions. He let his words land on the ears of his listeners, as they needed to hear them. He didn't force a political or social statement; he simply conveyed his experience in a real and honest way.

Honesty frees the speaker and attracts the audience.

A.W.E.S.O.M.E.

Casting director and producer, Ric Enriquez, describes honesty this way:

> I think the only way honesty appears, and it translates into everything, is when people stop being outside of themselves, watching themselves, and listening to themselves. They suddenly relax.
>
> In a television interview, a producer will normally ask some feeder questions, especially when the subject has never been on camera before. They ask questions to get them (the guests) comfortable and settled into the process, so you can lead them into telling the story.
>
> Once people get organically into the story, once you've found that groove, everything becomes real. They're now suddenly present. You see it in someone's eyes, you see it in their posture, and you see how they react when someone's listening.

Audiences look for this honesty. They want to know you are genuine in your approach and, if you are, that's when you have them. They listen to you and experience what you want them to experience. If you're not being honest, you lose your audience. They cease to listen.

Editor and director, Sharon Hashimoto, who studies people on video, points out how we, as audiences, know when someone is being authentic:

Magical

Sometimes people say one thing, but their face or body language says another. A lot of times, I see people saying one thing that's positive but they're shaking their head "No." I have a tendency to watch the body and think, "You're lying to yourself."

There is a fidgeting that happens, a playing with the hair, the playing with the nose, itchiness... because they usually feel uncomfortable about what they're saying, not necessarily on the surface, but subconsciously they know and so they start bringing attention to themselves. People may not know they're doing it, but the people that are watching definitely sense something is off.

Genuine honesty shows up in your entire being: your words, expressions, body gestures, and eyes. When you allow it to flow, others experience the real you more clearly. They are no longer searching for a connection. You've given it to them.

So what does this have to do with being magical? It's all part of creating your magical spell—an interactive communication experience that is unique and powerful.

Creating Something New

Public speaking, whether it is a pitch, a presentation, or a toast at a social engagement, is made up of multiple parts:

you (the sender), your audience (the receiver), the message, feedback, static, the environment, and the final part, which ties all of the first six together—the experience.

Communication Cycle Graphic

As the main player, your commitment to all these elements breathes into existence an experience that did not exist before. It starts with your idea. Its life begins before you even speak. Your attitude, approach, research, and preparation all play a role in how you show up and initially introduce the message. Once you speak it into the world, it's no longer just yours. It is shared with others.

How you continue to manage and choreograph the communication exchange determines whether a magical experience or an ordinary experience takes place.

Magic happens when you are:
 aligned to your expressive self,
  wired to your surroundings,
   empathetic with your audience,
    simple in your approach,
     and *open* to the experience.

When you are honest and relaxed, you can be in the moment and in flow. You are creative, an expert, and instinctively know what to do. You can let go of control and embrace your *fearFULL* power. When that happens, you can take your audience from one place to another. You can stimulate, inspire, or transform them. Whichever it is, you've created a magical experience for them and for yourself.

Lesson Learned

Every public speaking experience is distinct and unique. While the content and intent may be the same from one to the next, the audience, situation, context, and overall environment are different every time. How you are in each experience matters. Take it all in and allow every single element to flow through you. Live honestly in that moment and you will be magical.

Summary

- You cannot recreate a moment. You can only create new ones. This applies to every pitch, talk, or presentation. Each one provides a new magical opportunity.

- Your honesty allows the audience to genuinely experience who you are. When the best of you is set free, you open yourself to creating magic. You are in flow, one with everything around you.

- If you are truly grounded, you become a conduit who can create something unique and special. To get grounded, ask yourself:

    o Who needs what I have?

    o What can I say to best express myself?

    o Where are my mind, heart, and intuition when I begin to speak? Am I aligned?

- When am I most connected to the environment and audience? Am I wired and empathetic?

- Why is this important now, in this moment?

- How am I most charismatic, impactful, and effective?

• Magic happens when you are no longer self-aware and become fully connected in the experience. It pulls the audience toward you. They want more of you and your irresistible offer.

Exercise

Can you identify magical moments? Often you feel them before you see them. Pick a talk you've never seen before. Try TED or another professional organization that posts their talks online. Or attend a new talk. As you listen to the speaker, ask yourself:

• Who needs/wants this talk?

• What did the speaker say or do that made this talk special and unique?

• Where in the presentation did the speaker shine?

• When did you decide you liked or disliked the content and delivery?

- Why did you like or dislike it?

- How would you change or adapt this talk?

After you've fully dissected this talk, consider the top three things that made it magical—or not.

Next, evaluate the last pitch, toast, talk, or presentation you gave. Ask yourself similar questions. What were the top three things that made it magical—or could have made it magical? What would you do differently? What would you do the same?

Compare your talk to the professional one, and consider what you've learned about creating magic.

Call to Action

Treat each new experience as an opportunity to be the best speaker possible. Connect to that moment and experience, be your honest self in it, and let the magic happen.

Practice the mantra: *"I am magical: my thoughts, ideas, and words create reality."*

CHAPTER 12
Engaging

When you are committed, you are engaged.

Audiences want something that is real and they need you to be real in delivering it. They yearn to be engaged with you and your message.

Being true to *who you are* and your expertise is vital any time you are called to present yourself or your ideas. It doesn't matter whether it's a pitch, a work presentation, keynote, or toast. Be direct and sincere. Believe in yourself and your abilities. When you commit to being present like this, you can better engage your audience.

Programming executive and media personality, Brian Balthazar, takes this into consideration when people pitch him a TV idea:

> We're looking for people who are authentically and genuinely in the business of doing what they do, and we want that story to be told in a very truthful way. The people that come in and say that they do something that they don't, or say they're more experienced than they are, or are not the most sincere version of themselves, are the ones that don't get through. Those people that come in and are truly themselves get our attention.

To engage an audience, you must first be fully engaged with your own message and yourself as the messenger. It's important to know your material, understand its relevance to your audience, and share it in an authentic way. Before you speak one word to others, ask yourself,

"Do I truly believe in myself and my subject matter? Is my message honest, heartfelt, and generous?"

To engage an audience, you must also have conviction. People know immediately whether you're being sincere or disingenuous. Your authenticity is what attracts others to your message. Therefore, be credible in your approach, thoroughly committed to your purpose, and of service to those listening to you.

Here's an example of a speaker who fully committed to being his authentic self and, as a result, engaged his audience in such an inspiring way.

The Lawyer

When I first met him, I was surprised to discover he was a lawyer. A nice, friendly guy, he didn't seem to fit a stereotype of the "buttoned-down" attorney. I would soon discover that this young man had much to offer.

He revealed in his AWESOME TALK submission video that he was a competitive triathlete. A fit guy, it was easy to imagine him running, swimming, and biking. Little did Emily or I know at the time, this hadn't always been the case.

When we met him, he revealed to us that he actually didn't know how to swim when he decided to compete in his first triathlon. We already knew he was ambitious by going to law school, but this was a whole other level of dedication. Can you imagine signing up for a competition in which you have to run, bike, and swim—and not knowing how to do one of those activities?

This immediately demonstrated his character: he was a passionate and ambitious risk taker. Even though he had been nervous about swimming all his life, it was not enough to learn how to do it as an adult. He wanted to master it.

To accomplish this goal, he promised to practice, whether his technique was accurate or not, every day until he could swim like a pro—or at least be good enough to compete like one.

He had commitment. He was dedicated to overcoming his fear of swimming and doing it well enough to actually compete in his new sport. In the end, his practice paid off. He learned how to swim and competed in the triathlon. He reached his goal, even in the face of seemingly insurmountable challenges (not being able to swim).

This conviction also showed up when the lawyer prepared for the AWESOME TALK. His goal was to motivate others with his story. He aspired to be his best, both personally and professionally. That was the theme of his talk.

He began by sharing the lofty goals of competing in a

triathlon and then explained how he took a risk—he faced his fear of swimming—and learned to swim in just three months. After revealing this and how he prepared for the race, he shared his future ambitions of competing in national and international races.

At the AWESOME TALK, he was a bundle of energy from the moment he ran out on stage. He was spirited and upbeat. Keeping up this level of enthusiasm is not easy for most of us, yet for him, it seemed effortless.

We witnessed how his enthusiasm and passion to achieve was a driving force for him. This sort of energy is not only inspiring, it is contagious.

He was authentically passionate about life. This showed up in his story, the way he presented it, and how the audience reacted. They adored him.

Harness your Internal Power

The power of positivity is contagious. You motivate others to be their best when you declare your quest to be your best. This includes sharing your goals and accomplishments, as well as your struggles and learning. Your willingness to express imperfection is the perfect way to connect with and influence others.

Programming executive Loren Ruch, who develops and

oversees TV programming, believes that good ideas come to life when you believe in them, and that attitude is everything:

> If you come with a positive attitude, belief in the project, and you feel inside like there's something really great there, you're going to come across with a bigger smile, a more natural approach, and enthusiasm.

> People are always telling me that I'm very enthusiastic in my pitches. I'm not enthusiastic about everything in the world, but if I'm going to back something, I'd better be enthusiastic about it!

> You should not pitch anything that you do not believe in. Sometimes people pitch things and I let them know, "This isn't right for our brand, and I really appreciate the time" and they agree. "Yeah, we didn't think it was right either."

> Then, I wonder to myself, "Why are you putting your own self behind this?" If something doesn't feel right, then it's probably not right.

Conviction is not only attractive, it is essential for success in public speaking. When you believe wholeheartedly in your subject, you engage the audience on a deeper level. They can begin to feel what you feel, hear what you hear, and see what you see. You communicate with your entire being because it's not just a thought you are sharing—it's a belief you are expressing.

A.W.E.S.O.M.E.

When you're fully committed to an idea or project and are able to express it with sincere conviction, then you create a powerful call to action. Your audience is moved and, as a result, you can inspire, sell, convince, transform, or create many other possible reactions.

If you lack conviction, don't speak. Pretending to be something you're not is too great a risk. You will lose your audience's respect and damage your reputation. And both of them are hard to regain.

Positivity, passion, and conviction are building blocks for creating influence and engaging audiences. The key is that they are authentically you. Positivity is not about smiling and saying nice things so people like you. That can actually turn people off. Positivity is the ability to see possibilities. When there is doubt, you can offer a solution or see an alternative.

Positivity is a key element of Guiding Principle #1: you are creative. When you are positive, you are working towards a creative outcome. You harness your power to materialize a desired result. Add passion and conviction to this effort and you, yourself, are incredibly influential.

So where do you find your own influential power? Look within. You've had it all along. You just need to harness it.

Engaging

Your Public Identity

The lawyer was passionate, ambitious, and accomplished. These qualities served him when he went to law school, when he competed in triathlons, and also when he spoke. They were naturally ingrained in him. They appeared for others to see. They were part of his public identity.

Celebrities, TV personalities, and those in the entertainment business are well aware of their personas. Constantly under public scrutiny, they have no choice but to pay attention to how they come across. The success of their personal brands depends on it.

Positive and influential figures purposefully tap into their best qualities so they can show up well for their audiences. Professional speaker, girl empowerment expert, and author of *BeYOUtiful,* Julie Carrier actually pictures one individual and what that person needs to hear:

> I envision, "Who is the young woman that wants to hear this message?" I give her a name, imagine what she looks like, and then envision her face and eyes in the camera lens, so when I deliver that message, the person on the other side feels like I'm talking directly to her.
>
> I think the biggest challenge people have when it comes to being on television is they get so focused on the fact they're on TV that they forget to be authentic.

The camera gets in the way of them being themselves. Imagine the camera is not there or that the camera is your audience. Focus on them and that one person you want to speak to.

Whether you're onstage in front of five thousand people or in a small conversation that's being filmed to show to millions—it's the same principles.

You choose how you want to come across and how you want to engage your audience. Harness your shining light within. One way to bring out your best is to take stock of your unique qualities. Don't be shy. Identify those that make you feel confident, that describe how you want to be perceived as a speaker.

These qualities are the foundation of your celebrity quotient, your CQ. The core of your best self emerges, no matter the situation. The results will amaze you.

CQ, Your Celebrity Quotient

Emily and I first introduced the idea of your CQ in our first book *The Shining Unique You / Everyday Celebrity*. Your CQ (Celebrity Quotient) is the measure of your "Celebrity Essence" as designed, developed, and managed by you. It starts with identifying three characteristics that authentically and powerfully describe your personality. These characteristics are innate and natural, and are consistently revealed in your public identity. For example:

A leading actor/actress might be characterized as:

1) Good looking
2) Charming
3) Influential

A TV host might be described as:

1) Witty
2) Inquisitive
3) Personable

These two personalities show up differently. They each make a distinct impression. This impression is not based on a one-time experience. It is consistently experienced over time. In order to maintain their reputations and continue to build respect with their audiences, celebrities have to be consistent in how their CQs are revealed—in interviews, social media, and public appearances.

This is also true of us as individuals, professionals, experts of our irresistible offer, and speakers. We can be engaging in a consistent fashion, especially if we know our strengths.

Another way to think about your CQ in regard to your A.W.E.S.O.M.E. self is that they are the keywords for your personal brand. For example, with the lawyer, those keywords were:

- Passionate, Ambitious, and Accomplished

A.W.E.S.O.M.E.

For others, CQ keywords might be:

- Witty, Direct, and Bold
- Smart, Energetic, and Helpful
- Earnest, Sincere, and Giving

Through your CQ, you are able to track and maintain the way you want to come across to your audience.

- It is a road map for communication delivery and engagement.
- It informs your actions, what to wear, what to say, how to say it, and in what context.
- It is the core of your natural charisma and, once identified, it can be purposefully used to showcase your true innate star quality.

Your IQ and EQ (Intelligence and Emotional Quotient) are measures that help inform and guide you, each in their own way. Your CQ—Celebrity Quotient—is another tool. It is a way to design and manage how you want to show up in the world when you are called to present in front of others.

Defining your own CQ takes your passion and conviction and packages them in a way that is uniquely you. The three words you choose to describe yourself help you to fashion what you say, stay true to who you really are, and be engaging as your best possible self.

Lesson Learned

Every time you speak in public, you reveal what you think about yourself, your value, and your abilities. It is important to listen to your internal dialogue. Know with certainty that what you offer is a gift to those listening to you and allow the best you possible to show up in that moment. Be purposeful in your communication. Identify your personal CQ and allow it to be your guide for how you engage others.

Summary

- People are attracted to authenticity and know immediately when someone is being disingenuous. Your individuality is what they will connect with, appreciate, and remember.

- A speaker is of service to the audience. Have faith in your personal expertise, your emotional connection to the subject, the value it has to the audience, and the ultimate goal you wish to achieve.

- Get into the right mindset before you speak. Be positive, the best you possible in that moment, and allow yourself to be a conduit.

- Shine from within, using your celebrity quotient (CQ), the measure of your "Celebrity Essence" as designed, developed, and managed by you. Identify three characteristics that authentically and power-fully describe your best self.

Exercise

Do you know your CQ? It's time to find out and test it.

Take a moment to reflect on your skills and attributes. Then write down ten qualities that you feel best express *who you are*. Here are a few examples: friendly, passionate, smart, kind, ambitious, entertaining, straightforward, sincere, witty, creative, deep, insightful, and helpful.

Once you've identified your ten, talk to two people who know you well and ask them to pick their top three. Be open to other possibilities as well, in case they feel strongly that there's a quality that is not listed.

Next, introduce yourself to two new people whom you've never met before. Talk with them for five minutes, sharing a little bit about yourself and ask them to give you feedback on their top three picks.

After you've looked at the responses, pick your top three. Use these as your CQ for the next couple of weeks and see how it works. Do these traits really communicate the best you possible? Are they genuine? Do they produce positive results?

Note: If you've already done your CQ from our first book, *Everyday Celebrity*, please try this exercise again. It is dynamic and may change.

Call to Action

Believe in yourself and your message, and others will, too. Have conviction in your expertise and your ability to engage the audience in a way that is authentically you.

Practice the mantra: *"I step into my greatness and empower others to do the same."*

QUOTABLE MENTIONS ABOUT BEING A.W.E.S.O.M.E.

The following are thoughts and advice on being open, magical, and engaging.
What entertainment professionals say about being...

OPEN

"Public speaking is a conversation. If someone believes it is "I talk, you listen," then there's going to be disconnect."
- Julie Carrier,
  Girl's Empowerment
  Speaker

"Building a character and saying lines that someone else has written is vastly different from writing something personal and expressing it publicly."
- Michael Medico,
  Professional Actor
  and TV Director

"Know your material and go in prepared. And remember to be open-minded because the result may not be what you planned; it just might be better."
- Loren Ruch,
  TV Programming
  Executive

MAGICAL

"To truly connect with people, we have to give our true self on stage... and that vulnerability leaves us open to moments of unexpected magic."
- Jess Weiner,
  Self-Esteem Expert
  Speaker, and Actionist

"Wisdom lives inside the person. My job as a speaker is to activate that wisdom."
- Rick Tamlyn,
  Speaker, Author,
  and Coach

"It comes down to confidence. People can smell fear. They get a sense right away if you're nervous or intimidated."
- Mishawn Nolan,
  Entertainment Attorney

ENGAGING

"You buy a magazine based on its cover and layout. What's inside will get you to buy it again, but what makes you grab it off the shelf is the packaging."
- Zachary Bilemdjian,
  Costumer and Stylist

"You just have to learn and realize that whoever you truly are is who you need to be."
- Shahnti Olcese Brook,
  Producer and
  Talent Manager

"It's easy to make people cry. It's hard to make them laugh."
- Angelo Tsarouchas,
  Professional Comedian

SECTION IV:

A.W.E.S.O.M.E. Talk

CHAPTER 13

Tell Your Story

Make it personal and you've made it powerful.

When it comes to speaking, the biggest, most difficult step is not the one you take getting on stage for a presentation in front of hundreds of people. It's not the one you take walking into a meeting with your boss to ask for a raise. It's not the one you take standing up to deliver the eulogy of a love one.

The biggest step is the one you take deciding whether or not to even engage in an act of public speaking in the first place.

This seemingly simple decision is actually a challenging one. Multiple emotions, expectations, past experiences, and insecurities factor into it. Public speaking, whether the topic is about you or something else, is a personal pursuit. That's why we've focused so much attention on getting the A.W.E.S.O.M.E. YOU ready.

When you are **a**ligned, **w**ired, **e**mpathetic, **s**imple, **o**pen, **m**agical, and **e**ngaging, you no longer simply deliver a message. You *become* the message. You are a conduit to an irresistible offer. You are a storyteller at your best.

Now it's time to awaken your A.W.E.S.O.M.E. TALK—to be the best you possible each and every time you are handed the microphone, literally and metaphorically. Shine not just for one talk—a specific pitch, keynote, or toast— but show up as your powerful self *every* time you want to be impactful.

A.W.E.S.O.M.E.

You start by owning the fact that every public speaking opportunity is a personal journey. Here's an example of one speaker who mastered this quest.

The Travel Agent

A workaholic, the travel agent spent much of his time on the road with clients. This meant he often missed family events, like his wife's birthday. While he may not have been present at some of these gatherings, his heart was always there with his loved ones. In fact, the reason he worked so much was to provide a good life for his wife and kids.

His love and devotion to his family were the focus of his AWESOME TALK. He knew the story he wanted to tell and was committed to making it a powerful one for the audience. He first introduced this theme in his submission video.

The travel agent was a big guy with an even larger presence. You noticed him when he walked into the room. It might have been because of his height, loud voice, or bold personality, but you couldn't miss him. At the same time, he had an unusual tenderness, especially when he spoke about his family.

He learned to embrace both of these qualities as a speaker. He took what might be an intimidating quality—his size—and made it an endearing one by allowing the audience to also see a different side of him—his tenderness. This required a conscious choice on his part, to be vulnerable about his feelings.

As we worked with him on his talk, he decided to take another bold action. He wanted the audience to witness an apology to his wife. During his talk, he pulled out a card and it was a certificate for a trip she had always wanted to take. He knew, though, that he was giving her much more than a vacation. He was giving her his time and attention, which she wanted more than anything.

Why did he decide to share this deeply personal moment with the audience? He wanted to inspire other workaholics like him to do something for their loved ones. He knew he was a conduit with a powerful message, and chose to make the moment count.

The audience loved it. It came as no surprise that he was the winner of the very first AWESOME TALK.

Storytelling

The travel agent seamlessly meshed his professional and personal backgrounds into a relatable experience. As a result, his personal narrative was of service to those listening. He was a gift to his audience.

He was also a phenomenal storyteller with a very effective approach—because when a large man with an even bigger heart reveals personal vulnerability, you are compelled to listen to him. You pay attention.

What gifts or attributes do you have that draw people to you? In what ways do you optimize your CQ when speaking in public? In what ways do you create a narrative that has highs with dramatic peaks, and lows with subtle thought-provoking insights?

The travel agent addressed these questions, which provide two valuable reminders about storytelling:

1. Be of service to your audience. Your personal narrative or observations offer insight, inspiration, knowledge, or something else they didn't have before.

2. Be compelling in your approach. If something is important to you, then it will most likely be important to others.

Your abilities as a storyteller build on these ideas. It's important to make your story applicable and relatable. The experience may be your own, but the results of what happened and hindsight perspective are gifts you can give the audience. Take time to flesh out the lesson with a useful anecdote—and its benefit to those listening. Audiences are hungry for it.

Programming executive, Loren Ruch, who develops and oversees television series, points out that storytelling is everything:

Tell Your Story

If you can't tell a good story, I'm not going to trust you to produce a television show. Enthusiasm is part of storytelling. Passion for what you do is part of storytelling. Good writing is part of storytelling. It's all part of it, but ultimately, if you can't tell a story, you're not going to make good television.

Enthusiasm, passion, and good storytelling are important for all mediums of communication, including you as a speaker. Just ask media personality, self-empowerment expert, and professional speaker, Jess Weiner:

Great speakers, for me, are great storytellers. They approach every speech as an opportunity to take an audience through a thrilling narrative, no matter the topic. Part of storytelling is crafting a great format for your speech: enticing the audience with a killer hook, building the arc until you've hit them with a climactic key point or game-changing principle, and then leaving them with a clear call to action at the end. But the other part of storytelling is passion. You can't teach passion; it just flows from a person.

Indeed, great speakers are great storytellers. They keep it brief and powerful. When in doubt about your own storytelling skills, go back to the basics. Every story has three parts:

- Beginning
- Middle
- End

A.W.E.S.O.M.E.

If you miss a detail along the way, it's okay. Only you will know. It's the overall message and impact that's important to your audience. Keep that objective in mind and remember when you speak, you are a medium for something much greater: a story that is no longer just your own. Get clear and S.I.T. with your intention—are you going to stimulate, inspire, or transform others?

Remember to stay focused on your audience. Be of service to them and be compelling in your approach. To help you achieve these two goals, consider these questions:

- What does the audience need from me?
- What is the gift that only I can give them?
- How am I going to reveal this gift to them in a way that will reach them?

Keep these in mind as your speaking journey takes flight and they will help you face potential obstacles, including those that are self-inflicted.

Speaking Traps

In addition to forgetting a detail in a story, other mishaps, such as an environmental factor, might present an obstacle when you are sharing your story. Sometimes the disruption is dramatic and distracting. Other times it may be light and funny. Navigating the appropriate response at the right moment makes all the difference.

Media personality and programming executive, Brian Balthazar, describes the effects of a disruption:

> Once I let go and learned to relax a little bit, I stopped getting nervous. I got better. Also, I was more able to see things happening in the moment and react to them.

> It's amazing how many times, if someone's giving a speech and a light falls down offstage, they just keep going… There's a lighthearted moment to be seized. If something's happening, and it could be funny, just acknowledge it. Call out the moment.

When you are speaking, you are constantly in choice. Do you ignore mishaps or "call out the moment" for greater impact, like Brian says? When you make a mistake, do you segue to another topic or "go for the save" as professional comedian, Angelo Tsarouchas, advocates?

When unexpected things happen, take two steps:

- First, don't freak out. Keep the bigger picture in mind. You are there to be of service to your audience.
- Second, be still and embrace what is happening. Be

present in the moment, and not in your head. As we've already established in one of the guiding principles, you instinctively know what to do. Listen to that internal voice, not the negative, stressed-out dialogue that can distract you from your greater purpose.

When you keep these steps and perspective in mind, a loud noise, a technical glitch, or an annoying audience member won't derail you. You're still okay, even though your personal story doesn't come out "right."

When you get into your head and feed your anxiety, a simple incident becomes much bigger than it needs to be. And sometimes your own head games can be a trap of their own, as TV editor and director, Sharon Hashimoto, points out with some of the on-air talent she's worked with:

> They're not exactly as present as they should be in the moment. They're usually thinking about the next thing they're going to talk about or they're going to be asked. They're analyzing what they're saying at the same time as they're speaking.

We can create traps just by our own thinking towards speaking and storytelling. Here are a few of them.

- **Word Traps:** Your focus on words consumes you. If you miss a word in your speech or presentation, it throws you off. This reliance on the words you use keeps you overly scripted. Instead, focus on themes or key talking points, so if you miss a word (or detail in your story) you are still on point.

- **Technical Traps**: You're overly reliant on a PowerPoint or other technical element in your presentation. If what you have to present depends solely on another medium, then you are not being an effective medium yourself. Make sure whatever you use enhances what you are going to say and that you are not trapped by that technology to make the point.

- **"Yes" Traps**: Your focus on what you believe the audience wants to hear takes over. You already have the audience's time and attention, so give them something valuable—**your** message—even if it challenges their current thinking. If you merely "yes" them, chances are they won't respect you. If a portion of them disagree with you, that's okay. Trying to please everyone dilutes your offer and your impact.

The A.W.E.S.O.M.E. YOU is ready. You don't need to do anything that you don't already know how to do. Get out of your own way. It is your own self-sabotaging behavior—whether that is overthinking a situation or not paying attention to what's really important—that can sink you.

Don't be afraid to be personal. Your story is powerful. Make it part of your A.W.E.S.O.M.E. TALK.

A.W.E.S.O.M.E.

Lesson Learned

Be bold: speak from your personal experience. Share your story and draw in your audience in a personal, compelling way. Stay focused and provide service to your audience, regardless of external or internal distractions. As a storyteller, you are a conduit and what you share is not just yours. It is a gift you give to others.

Take the lessons you've learned as the A.W.E.S.O.M.E. YOU, like keeping it simple and being open, and let your A.W.E.S.O.M.E. TALK take flight. Shine every time you need to. You are already an excellent public speaker.

Summary

- Always show up as the best you possible—not just one time for one talk, presentation, or pitch. Shine *every time* you need to be influential, persuasive, and impactful. That is being A.W.E.S.O.M.E.

- Public speaking is personal. Embrace it and share your experiences. Be a storyteller.

- When it comes to storytelling: (1) be of service to your audience and (2) be compelling in your approach.

- When faced with distractions or potential speaking traps remember: don't freak out. Instead, embrace what is happening. You instinctively know how to handle it.

Exercise

Identify a personal experience that you are currently struggling with or that you just dealt with recently. Outline the three main points of your story: the beginning, middle, and end. Next, pinpoint highs and lows in that story, the dramatic turning points.

Then take all of these—your three main points as well as your highs and lows—and create lessons or anecdotes that could be of service to your audience in a compelling way. Once you've done all these steps, create a presentation that is between seven and ten minutes in length.

Practice this presentation in front of two live audiences. Make sure they are audiences of at least five people you do not know. For example, solicit a community organization, school, or professional association. Also, make sure the two audiences are comprised of individuals who are different. For example, one group might be college students, while the other could be made up of mid-level managers.

For each presentation, prepare an assessment. This assessment should be broken into three parts.

1. On a scale of one to five, with five being the best, ask them to rate you on the following items:
   - Were you of service to them?
   - How compelling were you?

2. Write out and briefly describe all seven parts of A.W.E.S.O.M.E.—**a**ligned, **w**ired, **e**mpathetic, **s**imple, **o**pen, **m**agical, and **e**ngaging. If you need help, go back and review Section II. Ask the participants to identify the top two items they experienced in your presentation, as well as the two items they felt you could improve.

3. Ask for overall feedback on how influential, persuasive, or impactful you were in the presentation.

After you receive this feedback, go back to your presentation and isolate what changes you can make to it. We will enhance these in the next chapter.

You are on your way to having that A.W.E.S.O.M.E. TALK.

Call to Action

Be the A.W.E.S.O.M.E. YOU every time you speak in public!

Practice the mantra: *"I am A.W.E.S.O.M.E.— aligned, wired, empathetic, simple, open, magical, and engaging."*

CHAPTER 14
S.P.E.A.K.

Compelling speakers have a clear call to action.

When you put your audience and message first, you are of service. When you're personal and shine as your best self, you are compelling. When these two audience-focused elements are part of your content and delivery, your presentation becomes an A.W.E.S.O.M.E. TALK.

Everything you've done up to now has prepared you to show up as your best. Now let's turn our attention to one of my favorite questions, "For the sake of what?"

For the sake of what are we getting ourselves aligned, wired, and empathetic? For the sake of what are you simple, open, magical and engaging in your approach to public speaking?

The top three answers my coaching clients mention again and again? They want to be:

- *Influential*
- *Persuasive*
- and *Impactful*

Let's dig deeper. What does it take to achieve these outcomes when you speak?

Rick Tamlyn, author of *Play Your Bigger Game,* says it starts with a commitment:

A.W.E.S.O.M.E.

People say, "You have to be courageous, you have to be confident [when you speak in public]." For me, I don't know if I'm confident or courageous; what I am is committed. Put me in front of a room, put me in front of a person, put me in front of a workshop. I have an opinion about training this room because of my belief system and what I want for this room and my training. I'm committed.

When you want to be influential, persuasive, or impactful, be a committed storyteller and content creator. What's the difference? When you tell stories, you are sharing something personal in a compelling way. Even if it's not a personal story, you are giving your personal perspective on it.

As a content creator, you are formulating lessons, anecdotes, and information from those stories (and more) for the sake of creating a *call to action*. Your presentation or other form of public speaking is aimed at moving the audience in some direction. You are there to **s**ell, **p**romote, **e**ntertain, **a**ctivate, or **k**now—you are there to S.P.E.A.K.

S.P.E.A.K.

This acronym highlights five different focal points for your content: **s**ell, **p**romote, **e**ntertain, **a**ctivate, or **k**now. They are calls to action. They help you formulate what you are going to say.

For example, if your focus is to entertain your audience, then you will use different anecdotes and talking points than if your focus is to activate them. To better understand the differences between each of these foci, let's break them down.

Sell

When you *sell*, you are persuasive. Your goal is to create a transaction.

For example, you might be soliciting a group of investors for funding or seducing consumers to buy your product. Your talking points must clearly identify and express how you or your product addresses the needs of your audience. You present the problem and offer a solution — you provide an irresistible offer that the audience cannot deny.

Sales is a pervasive part of our lives, as casting director and producer, Ric Enriquez, points out:

> Everything in life is sales. The moment you accept that, the easier it is for you. There's no version of this, there's no side of the exchange that isn't a sale. Occasionally you get to be a buyer but, ultimately, that person is still selling something because if you're buying it, you're gonna turn around and sell it to the public.
>
> So the moment you accept that this is all sales, it helps

you tremendously. You just have to know your product, and sometimes your product is yourself. For me, my product is another actor, so I have to be comfortable selling this actor to my team of people. When I sold TV shows, I had to believe in the idea, and then I had to believe in the talent we put behind the idea. You're always selling.

You not only have to believe in the product, but you have to get those listening to you to believe in it, too. Present your content in a way that even the toughest critic will be in A.W.E.—aligned, wired, and empathetic—to your message. Go in prepared, engaged, and make a connection, as talent agent Tim Curtis recommends:

> Come across like you care: it's just sort of the confidence with which you walk into a room. Make initial contact in terms of speaking first, in terms of eye contact, in terms of smiling, in terms of all the body language that we've heard a hundred times before. It really does make a difference how you connect with people. If there is a personal connection off the bat, they're going to be more likely interested in what that person has to say.

Promote

When you *promote* or publicize, you are influential. Your goal is to create awareness and excitement.

S.P.E.A.K.

For example, you might be posting photos and information about your new company on social media or talking at a tradeshow about your brand. Your talking points and stories must be descriptive and relevant to your audience. You are there to introduce and pitch something to your audience that they may not know about and get them emotionally invested.

We're always pitching something, including ourselves, says TV programming executive Loren Ruch:

> I feel like you're always pitching yourself in your career. The first time you take a job interview, you're pitching yourself. I remember when I was looking for that first internship.

> Early on, I had to pitch myself. I was twenty-one years old when I got the job at *Love Connection* [a TV show]. I was a kid, but I convinced them I was capable of being in this contestant coordinator position, which seemed like a very large position to me at the time. I think part of it is just selling yourself with confidence. Good pitching starts with the way you pitch yourself.

Conviction about your product is definitely important, but so is listening to whether or not it is beneficial to your audience. If you're trying to promote something that is not relevant to what he or she wants or needs, don't force it. The listener just might even like you more and listen to you next time, just as Loren describes when he receives TV pitches:

I love when someone's first question is, "Tell me about your brand." Or, "Tell me what you're looking for" instead of going right into their pitch. If they're like, "What is it that works for you?" or "What are some of the shows that you look up to on your network?" Because then, the good pitchers will say, "You know, I brought something with me but I'm realizing it has the wrong tone. I'd like to come back in two weeks."

I love that person. That to me is not a sign of failure that their pitch didn't work. It's a sign of success that they're listening.

Entertain

When you *entertain* others, you are impactful. Your goal is to create some sort of emotional reaction from your audience.

For example, an audience might be delighted with laughter as you tell jokes at a local comedy club or smile as you share fond stories about your best friend at her wedding. Your stories and anecdotes should relate and connect to the lives of your audiences. You're providing catharsis, lightness, and even encouragement to those listening to you.

When you're entertaining an audience, you're breaking down barriers, as professional comedian, Angelo Tsarouchas, describes:

S.P.E.A.K.

A lot of people are funny and don't even know it. It doesn't have to be a full-on comedy routine, but I think a lot of times if you want to break the ice from monotony, it's nice to tell a joke about yourself; maybe be self-deprecating or share something that happened to you. Say something relatable that people will get a chuckle out of and say, "Okay."

When others relate to you in an entertaining way, it empowers them to see their own lives differently. Just ask media personality and TV programming executive, Brian Balthazar:

> I love an event or a speaking engagement that doesn't take itself so seriously, that you can have fun and laugh. So in speaking to groups, allow yourself to inject a little humor in it. Because truthfully, much of life is pretty ridiculous. What's important to the world sometimes—what is getting the most attention—is often not the most important thing. Being able to laugh at that, having humor, is so important. It can get you through the worst of times if you're able to find the smallest fraction of humor.

Humor is not the only kind of entertainment; however, it does serve as an example of how to approach an audience when you want to engage them in an entertaining way. You provide a unique outlook, tell a descriptive story, and solicit an emotional reaction.

A.W.E.S.O.M.E.

Activate

When you *activate* your audience, you are impactful and influential. Your goal is to motivate, mobilize, or unify them toward a personal or common goal.

For example, you might gather your staff to brainstorm a presentation or speak to a group of protestors about social injustice. Your talking points and stories must be passionate, credible, and relevant. You want to awaken others to their own and, at times, others' greatest potential.

Rick Tamlyn, author of *Play Your Bigger Game*, is an activational speaker who believes:

> People want to be activated to their own brilliance. "Activate me" is different than "motivate me." "Motivate me" has a claim where I'm supposed to motivate them, so it puts that pressure on me. "Activate" is I'm going to give you something to think about, and maybe you're going to turn to your neighbor and talk about, "Let's see what's activated in you." It [the idea of activating] lives inside a core belief I have: the wisdom, insight, and understanding of what we're all looking to grow into comes from inside ourselves.

When you activate others, you create powerful change. This change starts with each of us, but the potential is far greater, as self-esteem expert, author, and professional speaker, Jess Weiner, points out:

S.P.E.A.K.

An individual must commit to an internal, personal evolution before they can accomplish an external, public revolution. Big, revolutionary change requires emotionally healthy and resilient people and that comes through the journey of self-discovery. That journey is messy and full of hard work, but stepping into the mess is the greatest piece of advice that I could offer. You'll be a stronger storyteller when you can connect with your purpose and develop the self-confidence that comes from knowing yourself and your talents more deeply.

Know

When you *know* a subject or are an expert in it, you influence others. Your goal is to share this insight with your audience.

For example, you might be giving a makeup lesson at a local beauty salon or a marketing workshop at a business conference. Your talking points and stories must be clear, well organized, and informative. You want to inspire and educate others.

Belief in your own ability and knowledge is critically important. Marketing and communications executive, Jered Gold, advocates that you become a subject matter expert:

Know your subject matter. Know it backward and forward to the point where you *become* the expert. *Be* the expert. If you say that you are speaking on...telephone book etiquette, then be the expert on telephone book etiquette.

Truly knowing your subject is important because the audience knows if you're faking it, as entertainment attorney, Mishawn Nolan, points out:

I meet with a lot of creatives, and you can tell when they're talking about their creative strengths. They speak one way. They're very confident. They're very focused. They're very natural when they speak; if they go outside their comfort zone, there's like a heightened sense of anxiety. They sometimes get a little bit more aggressive. They get anxious and nervous because it's not their thing—they're not comfortable anymore.

It doesn't matter whether you are going to sell, promote, entertain, activate, or share your knowledge. Be a committed storyteller and content creator. Before you take the stage, answer the question, "Why am I here?"

To help you better understand how each of these objectives differ, take a look at this S.P.E.A.K. chart with specific calls to action (CTA).

S.P.E.A.K.

CTA	PURPOSE	LANGUAGE	RESULT
Sell	Persuasion	Your talking points must clearly identify and express how you or your product address the pain points or needs of your audience.	You present the problem and offer a solution–you provide an irresistible offer that the audience cannot deny.
Promote	Influence	Your talking points and stories must be descriptive and relevant to your audience.	You introduce and pitch something to your audience that they may not know about and get them emotionally invested.
Entertain	Impact	Your stories and anecdotes should relate and connect to the lives of your audiences.	You provide catharsis, lightness, and even encouragement to those listening to you.
Activate	Impact & Influence	Your talking points and stories must be passionate, credible, and relevant.	You awaken others to their own and, at times, others' greatest potential.
Know	Influence	Your talking points and stories must be clear, well organized, and informative.	You inspire and educate others.

A.W.E.S.O.M.E.

Lesson Learned

Be committed to your audience, subject matter, and call to action. When you combine this commitment with a compelling delivery, you are influential, persuasive, and impactful. You have an A.W.E.S.O.M.E. TALK. All the work you've done preparing yourself to be all you can be when the spotlight is on you has paid off. You are the message.

Summary

- Ask yourself, "Why am I here?"

- Effective speakers are: (1) good storytellers, who share personal experiences and lessons and (2) content creators, who organize these stories, lessons, and talking points to create a call to action.

- Take time to consider how you are going to S.P.E.A.K. Are you there to **s**ell, **p**romote, **e**ntertain, **a**ctivate, or **k**now? When you take time to look at these calls to action, you are a more effective content creator.

- Be committed in your approach to public speaking. Take the A.W.E.S.O.M.E YOU and combine it with a strong call to action, thoughtful storytelling, and well-developed content, and you have an A.W.E.S.O.M.E. TALK.

Exercise

Review the exercise in the previous chapter and the lessons you learned from your evaluation sheets. Now **add a clear call to action** to your presentation, which should be between seven and ten minutes. Consider what you want to S.P.E.A.K. about. Are you there to sell, promote, entertain, activate, or know?

With that in mind, prepare a new presentation with that focus. Go back to one of the groups you spoke to before and redo your presentation. How did this clearer focus change your talk?

If you're feeling really ambitious—try doing the same talk two different times, each time with a different focus and call to action. For example, try to sell in one talk and activate in another. What changes do you need to make? How do those changes make a difference to the talk and to you as a speaker?

Call to Action

Create content that is compelling and relevant to your audience. Ask yourself how you are going to speak to them. Are you going to sell, promote, entertain, activate, or know a subject that will make a difference to them? Once you decide, commit. Do it!

Practice the mantra: *"I am seen, heard, and powerful. When I speak, people listen."*

CHAPTER 15

More than "15 Minutes of Fame"

Keep the momentum going every time you speak.

If you've read everything up to now and done all the exercises, you're well on your way to sharpening your skills for engaging in A.W.E.S.O.M.E. talk. The challenge now is to sustain your learning through practice. Take these lessons and integrate them every time you speak publicly. The best way to enhance your speaking talents is through experiencing them in action.

Remember, it's not about an isolated moment in time. You're not preparing for just one single talk, presentation, or pitch. You are integrating the A.W.E.S.O.M.E. YOU anytime you express your thoughts and ideas in public.

In the entertainment business, there's a popular phrase, "Fifteen minutes of fame." Inspired by an Andy Warhol quote, "In the future, everyone will be world-famous for fifteen minutes," this phrase refers to short-lived notoriety. Some examples might include: a YouTuber who pulls a crazy stunt and gets some publicity for a couple of weeks, an actor who is criticized for being selfish, then donates his time for a worthwhile charity and looks good in the public's eye for a while, or a singer who has just one hit, often referred to as a "one-hit wonder."

Likewise, a speaker may gain attention or notoriety for a limited amount of time. For example, a speaker at a political rally who gets her audience charged up before a march, but is never heard from again after that day, or a personal toast a best man gives at a wedding, but the next day isn't prepared to speak at a work function.

A.W.E.S.O.M.E.

My wish for you is to be A.W.E.S.O.M.E. all the time. It's not just about an isolated experience. It's about sustaining positive momentum each and every time you speak.

Remember the lessons you've learned so far. And now, from entertainment insiders, here are fifteen tips on how to shine as a speaker when you need it most, and keep your momentum going.

15 Tips from 15 Entertainment Professionals

For making your impression last for more than just fifteen minutes...

Tip #1: Acknowledge you want it

> "I think that there needs to be a desire to entertain people, or at least have an audience. And there's a wanting to be liked, a wanting for approval. You have to have a little bit of those things. It doesn't necessarily mean that you're egomaniacal, but there has to be little components of that desire, whether you admit it to yourself or not."
>
> *– Sharon Hashimoto, TV Editor,*
> *Director and Producer*

Tip #2: Take a risk

"Put yourself out there in a meaningful way. In any aspect, whether that's in a relationship or at work, volunteer for something. Just step up and say, 'Hey, I'm here—what can I do to help?' I think that when you put yourself in that position, and are willing to do that, you automatically jump ahead three paces faster than someone who's not willing or able to do that because of their own fears. You'd be surprised that just by stepping forward and saying, 'Hey, let me try something,' or, 'Let me help you do this,' or 'I have a question,' is probably one of the greatest ways to step forward in life."

— Tim Curtis, Talent Agent

Tip #3: Put yourself out there

"Everything you say, everything you do, every gesture that you make, is being looked at. You're basically saying, 'Look at me, I have something important to say,' and then all of a sudden everybody's looking at you and you're like, 'Wait, why are you looking at me?' It's one of the most vulnerable things that you can do because all of a sudden, you're putting yourself out there saying, 'I have something important to say.' Then you have to follow it up with something important to say."

— Zachary Bilemdjian, Costumer and Stylist

A.W.E.S.O.M.E.

Tip # 4: Be authentic

"I can tell when someone's not being authentic. There are several indicators. If it's an area that I understand, I can tell because they're not using the right vocabulary, they are not using industry normative terms. You can tell if they are sort of over-bragging. You can tell they're overcompensating for who they are. You can tell and you can just smell when someone is confident about what it is they're doing and someone is real. I think you can tell when someone is sitting there, and just dripping in who they are."

— Mishawn Nolan, Entertainment Attorney

Tip #5: Be passionate

"You must find your 'must'—your joy and your passion. When you find those and make your public moments about expressing that which is of utmost importance to you, not worrying about the outcome but enjoying your moment of freedom and expression, you have the keys to your own kingdom, and the possibilities are limitless."

— Andi Matheny, Professional Actor
and Acting Coach

Tip #6: Find out what matters to you most

"I think from a marketing standpoint many of us get caught in the, 'What's the thing that's going to sell?' That's the wrong question. Instead think, 'What is the thing I'm here to talk about, and what is the thing that matters to me?"

We don't spend enough time being in that state of 'What *is* my thing? What is *my* message? What *matters* to me?... so much so that I'm willing to stand on a stage, or stand in front of a room, or turn it into a workshop or write a book about it.'"

– Rick Tamlyn, Professional Speaker,
Author and Coach

Tip #7: Get a comprehensive perspective

"Take a look at your subject from three different angles. First, do your research. The second part is talking to others, getting their perspective and asking them for their expertise. See what their experiences are. Then the third step is your own personal experience.

My personal relationship to a subject is going to inform me in a certain way, my research on a subject is going to inform me in another way, and talking to other people in the field is going to inform me in a third way. All three angles are valuable.

If I say the sky is blue because I've experienced it, because the research I've done tells me that it's blue, according to XYZ, and I've also talked to person A, person B, and person C, and they've also said that it's blue, then it's most likely blue."

– Jered Gold, Marketing
and Communications Executive

Tip #8: Claim your opinion

"Claiming your opinion as something that you believe in is a little bit scary. We're so used to living in a world where you're trying to accommodate everybody, be a people pleaser, and get the message that everyone wants to hear. When you're asked point-blank what your opinion is and where you stand on something, it's a little scary to dive deep and come up with what you truly believe and stand by it.

I think that's one of the lessons for me that over the past five years or so, I've really claimed my own beliefs, and I realize that I'm getting more respect from people, not less. They might not always agree with me, but they like that I have a richer and deeper conviction with what I'm talking about."

– Loren Ruch, TV Programming Executive

Tip #9: Know how and when to prepare

"When I have an interview for a client or I have an event for a client and they need to speak in front of people, I don't prep them too far in advance because I think it makes them a little cuckoo and nervous. I like to do it as close to the event as possible, because then what I find is they are able to take it in.

I've watched this happen time and time again... a lot of high-profile celebrities and actors, writers, directors, authors—when they're so busy trying to get ready for their event, they're doing ten different things, and they're jumping from something to something. The last thing they want to do is remember: When is the movie coming out? Where am I going to be next week? What am I doing? And if I can literally feed that information to them right before they jump in, especially if they're actors, it's a lot easier for them to take it and kind of make it their own."

– Amy Prenner, Entertainment Publicist

Tip #10: Make it Personal

"If anybody has to get up to speak, for whatever reason, I always say: tell us a little bit about yourself. Not your life story, but if you can tell us something about yourself in a little bit of a funny way... it could be a personal experience, or a little story, or something that happened to you that morning, even if it didn't happen that morning. I think every speaker should make it a little personal.

– Angelo Tsarouchas,
Professional Comedian and Actor

Tip #11: Accept that you are nervous

"You're one person at home, and you're another person at work, because you kind of notice that you *have to be* or you choose to be. What a lot of people want to be is the same person, but you have a different comfortability when you're at home than maybe when you're out in the public.

One of the things I tell people, including different influencers or talent that might be feeling a little shy or insecure is: We're all just people. Everybody's nervous, everybody has anxiety, everybody is a little self-conscious about what they're doing, and nobody is judging you. You're probably judging yourself more than anyone else is."

– Shahnti Olcese Brook, Talent Executive,
Celebrity Booker and Manager

Tip #12: Practice your talking points out loud

"Saying something in your head versus saying it out loud is never the same. You think in your head. When you're thinking out loud, you're correcting yourself faster than real time. In your head, you may have this perfect delivery, but until you say it out loud, you don't really know how it's going to come out. So, once I feel like I can do that with those bullet points, I'll do it again, a couple more times. But then I try to do it once without the cards."

– Brian Balthazar, TV Programming Executive and Media Personality

Tip #13: Confront your fears

"Just like any other fear, the fear of presenting our ideas has to be confronted head-on. Terrified to speak up in company brainstorming sessions? Volunteer to lead the next one! Paralyzed by stage fright? Sign up to speak at your child's next PTA meeting! Whenever we are pushing ourselves past our fear, it can focus us on our own inner growth. It builds the relationship you have with yourself and makes it stronger.

The most important thing to remember is that you cannot let your fears hold you hostage. You must recognize opportunity and respond when it knocks. You have to jump on the moments that terrify you because life rewards you for it. Those moments of vulnerability are all important parts of our journey of self-discovery. Plus, the ideas that you allow yourself to speak into existence could be the key to unlocking a new skill or talent!"

– Jess Weiner, Media Personality, Speaker,
and Self-Esteem Expert

Tip #14: Make eye contact

"In America, one of the ongoing tips is, 'Imagine your audience not wearing clothes.' Another tip was, 'When you're talking to your audience, don't actually look them in the eye; look above their heads at the back of the wall, in the back of the room.' Those are the worst pieces of advice because your audience knows if you're looking at them. Your audience knows if you're feeling a connection with them.

So, the way I look at it is, rather than putting yourself in the mindset of, 'Oh, I'm going to give this speech to all of these people,' put yourself in the mindset that 'I'm going to have a conversation with one person.'

And what do I mean by that? For example, when I'm on stage, I actually look at one person each time that I'm getting ready to start a new sentence. So, I look at one person, and I'm talking to them. And then I shift my gaze and I look at another person, and so even though the audience might be a thousand people, or five hundred people, I'm actually having lots of individual conversations with that whole audience.

Here's the beauty of it: when that one person feels like you're looking just at him/her, everyone else in the audience feels that connection, even though you may not be looking them in the eyes. It's actually a whole way to shift the tone and the energy of your presentation. Put yourself in the mindset that, "I'm going to have lots of conversations with one individual," like one person, one person, one person, one person, as opposed to, 'I'm talking to this massive audience all at once!' And that shifts the energy in the room."

– Julie Carrier, Professional Speaker,
Girls Empowerment Expert, and Author

Tip #15: Speak from the heart

"I find what works for me about speaking is what I admire in other speakers. I always try to speak from my heart. My gut. I don't try to be clever. That doesn't mean I don't add humor. Humor is in my gut. But I don't try to sound smart or clever. I try to take the focus off me and put it on: What is my goal? To inspire? To teach? To relate? To touch? To give assurance or comfort?

And then, I let *anything* I want to say show up on the

page. I may edit it down later, but at first I just let I flow. After it's all written down, I do another pass on it, reminding myself to keep it simple, always making sure that my stories don't get away from me or the point. I want to make sure that everything is on track with my purpose.

I really love it when someone is prepared but when they go to speak, they get their head out of the page and just speak. I love it when a speech is conversational and feels very personal. I don't care if they said every word they wrote. I don't care if they stumble. Do they have something personal to say and are they present? That is where the gold lies."

– Michael Medico, Professional Actor
and TV Director

SECTION V:

Be the Message

CHAPTER 16

Self-Declarations, Perceptions, and Assessments

What you see in yourself may not be nearly as powerful as what others see in you.

Your ability to be an effective public speaker has been a part of you for a very long time. It began years ago—long before you even realized that you were being a "speaker." For example, when you successfully persuaded your parents to let you stay up late or influenced your classmates to play a certain game, you were practicing how to be compelling speaker.

At an early age, you began to explore the power of your expressive being, using your words, intention, and conviction to get what you wanted. Since then, you have been developing these communication assets your entire life.

You are already powerful in your own unique, wonderful way. That's a given. What I've had the pleasure to do is to provide you a framework or model on how to harness and trust your power as a public speaker.

Go back to the seven elements of what it means to be A.W.E.S.O.M.E. and the three guiding principles: (1) you are creative, (2) you a subject matter expert, and (3) you instinctively know what to do. When you do, you tap into the best expressive you possible. You can also better engage situational and environmental factors that might impact you as a speaker.

Some of these factors you originate and others are imposed on you. They are self-declarations, perceptions, and assessments. Being able to identify and understand them gives you that extra, final edge to be the speaker you know you can be!

First Impressions

We tell the world what to think of us. We share our point of view about others, the world, and ourselves all the time. One way we do it is through our style choices, grooming, attitude, and our approach. Before we open our mouths, people feel that they know us. We make an impression. And even if they get it wrong, their judgments about us affect whether they are open or closed to what we have to say.

Your first impression sets you up for success or a struggle. Talent agent Tim Curtis describes "first impression" as follows:

> If someone doesn't make a good first impression when they walk into a room, they can still give a great pitch, and maybe the pitch is so strong it'll turn things back around, but it's a struggle. Once you start spiraling down, it's tough to recover. You can usually feel the energy in a room, whether it's going well or not going well. And if you start feeling that it's not, then you've got to figure out how to bounce back and pull everyone on board again, or else just end the meeting because it's pointless from that moment forward.

Self-Declarations, Perceptions, and Assessments

The moment we see someone, we create a story about him or her and an assessment about that individual's value to us. Is he or she someone worth my attention and time? It's almost instinctual, as TV editor and director, Sharon Hashimoto, points out:

> I think people really do profile—and I'm not saying people are shallow—I think that people automatically will profile you based off of the way you look and how you present yourself to the world.

Appearance

How do you take control of the impression you want to make? Take a look at your clothing and grooming choices. What you wear and how you appear says a lot. Your attitude about yourself, others, and being in public is communicated visually and this has a tremendous influence on how people listen and respond. Stylist and costumer, Zachary Bilemdjian, describes the role of appearance:

> I think people subconsciously or consciously have formed an opinion about you before you even open your mouth based on the way you look. You make an impression just by walking into the room.

> Dress how you want people to think of you. For example, if you want people to think of you as

intelligent, well-dressed, creative, avant-garde or any other buzzword, you have to dress the part.

Every day you make conscious choices on how to present yourself. You may dress to impress, as artistic expression, for comfort, or a myriad of other reasons. When it comes to speaking in public, what choices do you make about your wardrobe? What do you communicate about yourself almost immediately when you pitch, facilitate a workshop, or give a toast?

Do your clothes and attitude match what you are speaking about? Zachary has thoughts you may want to consider:

> One thing that I think is important is that if someone asked, "Okay who is the most authoritative person in this room?" They should be able to scan the room and identify you. And if there's a dispute, they're like, "Oh yeah. He's going to be able to help us because he looks like he's someone who would have the answer to that."

> To me, confidence is polished. I think confidence comes from being prepared. If you're walking into a board meeting, prepare yourself for it. It's a mindset. You go into it saying, "I know this. I got this."

Is the "I got this" attitude expressed in all you do—from your wardrobe to your attitude and message? Remember, it's not just about words when you speak publicly. It's about your comprehensive presence. You communicate a definite message visually. Take time to build your brand— the identifying characteristics you want to be remembered by. Go back to your CQ and evaluate whether the way you look represents the way you choose to come across. You have a choice—make it count.

Point of View

Your point of view shapes your stories and talking points when you are speaking. It reveals your approach to life and the world. If you're closed off and guarded, it shows. The audience, in turn, closes off and tunes out.

If you have a unique outlook in your storytelling, the audience pays attention. You increase your opportunity to be impactful because they are intrigued by what you reveal.

Find your distinct voice and let it be heard. Comedians do this quite well. Take a look at this story from professional comedian, Angelo Tsarouchas, and how his outlook and approach help him be engaging:

> I always tend to pick out the funny situations. It could be a funeral. It could be a baptism. It could be a birthday. I'll just see something funny, like why is this person doing this?

A.W.E.S.O.M.E.

At my own father's funeral in Canada, there were these three old women in the corner all dressed in black. So my mom and my aunt asked me, "Do you know who those women are?" and I said, "No, let me go over and talk to them. Maybe they were friends of dad's way before we knew?"

I went over and said, "Hello, I'm Angelo. I'm Peter's son. Did you guys know my father?"

They responded, "No. Our sympathies for your father."

Then, I went to the funeral director and asked, "What's the deal?"

He said, "They're funeral groupies."

"What do these people do?" I asked him and he said, "Oh, they come every week, every funeral. They just show up."

Now tell me, is that not funny? It's not funny that my father died. It's unfortunate, God rest his soul. But it's funny that there are *funeral groupies.*

They're in the neighborhood and they just show up. They grieve. They look like your aunties, your grandmas. They're nice ladies and you're not going to say, "Get out!" That's not what we do. If I was to pick a place to hang out, I don't think I would pick a funeral

264

parlor. But for them, it's better than going to Starbucks or Coffee Bean.

I told my brother and my sister. "So, they don't know Dad?" they asked.

I said, "No."

"Do they know Mom or anybody?"

"No, they are probably widows themselves and they just want to hang out. Maybe because it makes them feel [better]. Maybe they miss their family." We had a chuckle and I said, "If my father was alive, he'd laugh at this, too. He'd say, 'Well, let them have some cognac and some cheese.'"

I'll take stories like that and I'll sit on them. I've had people tell me their story situations—not trying to be funny. I'll be sitting there listening to them and I kind of giggle a bit and they'll go, "You think that's funny?" Then I go, "Do you think it's funny?"

"I never looked at it from that angle."

I say, "Everything you're telling me is funny, but you don't realize what's going on here. You're on the anger side of it so you're not seeing the funny part of it. You're distressed or upset. But I see the funny part of it."

Maybe as an outsider, I can look in better than they do. It is a matter of perspective because a lot of times something can happen to you and you don't think it's funny. But then a month later you're sitting around with friends and you say it again, then all of a sudden you're like, that was a little strange, wasn't it?

The next time you speak, take a moment to look at what point of view you communicate through your stories. Can you add humor? Offer a different twist to a situation? Do you express something the audience will value and connect to? If not, take a moment to re-evaluate what you can do differently.

Digital Footprint

One way you engage in public speaking is via social media. You communicate and express your point of views and ideas via your posts, tweets, images, or videos. The communication dynamic works just the same in this media as it does for speaking live—there is a sender, receiver, message, static, context, and (specialized digital) environment.

Even though you don't always physically talk, except maybe when you post a video, you are using your voice. You show up and present *who you are* or want others to believe *who you are*. You have an online identity and, based on that, good or bad, others perceive you a certain way.

Self-Declarations, Perceptions, and Assessments

We all live on the stage of public opinion. So, pay attention to how you communicate your thoughts and emotions, express your brand, and present your view of the world, especially when using social media. Don't be fake or insincere; just be aware. If you have a strong opinion and want to state it, know there may be backlash.

Keep in mind rules of online etiquette. Would you demean others if you were speaking from the stage? Probably not, so why even consider doing it online? If that's your brand, fine, but it's not very conducive to drawing people to you or your message.

You can do better. Be creative. It's not just influencers who have hundreds of thousands or millions of followers that should pay attention. Each of us leaves a lasting impression. What we say online stays online forever.

If you want to maintain a certain image, pay attention to what you put out on social media, as entertainment publicist, Amy Prenner, advocates:

> You have to be very careful that the image you want to convey is something that's respectable and not controversial so that people will want to follow you and be able to peel back the layers and learn more about you.

It's easy to sit behind a laptop, tablet, or phone and say whatever you want. Often, people express themselves in a way that they wouldn't do face to face, either because they're too scared to say it or simply lack the social skills. Ask yourself, would you say the same thing online that you would in another public platform?

Shahnti Olcese Brook, celebrity booker and talent manager, challenges us to consider this scenario:

> People will say and do a lot of things from behind a computer. But then once you have to speak in person, and it doesn't even need to be in front of a crowd, it could just be shaking another person's hand, it's nerve-racking. A lot of really amazing influencers that I talk to and work with, they all say that. That they're not used to interacting with people. When they meet and interact in person, they get very anxious. They know they're anxious and just need a little bit of help because like they all say, 'I'm used to being in my room by myself, interacting with the world in my corner', so it's a big difference.

Social media is social currency. As a professional, it's not a matter of whether or not you engage, but how you engage. It's part of your identity, and I firmly believe that if you are not in control of the message about you, someone else might be. So, as Amy says, take control:

> The number one thing that I probably would not have said a decade ago that is more important than PR— and before you ever think to hire a publicist—is to look

at your social media footprint and see how visible you are. If I had a dollar for every time I told somebody to work on your social media, I would be a multi-millionaire because social media measurements are important for lots of different things within the industry.

Social Attitudes

One of the ways you make an impression on others is your background. In this instance, it is nothing you necessarily say or do, but merely who you are. It's about the person listening to you and his or her biases. They may have judgments about you for a myriad of reasons, including your age, education, social status, sexual orientation, belief system, religion, ethnic background, and more.

So what can you do about these biases? First, be aware of them. Second, look for the connection, not the differences you have with that group or person. Another person's assessment of you is static in the communication cycle, and like other forms of static, it can be addressed with the right approach.

Marketing and communications executive, Jered Gold, knows firsthand what this is like:

> When I first started working at Art Center, I would do presentations for social groups, like the Elks Club. I just had to get out of my own head and not worry

about how these people were going to view me. You walk into these situations and there are all those concerns: I'm too young, I'm too liberal, I'm too Jewish, I'm too gay, I'm too whatever. You're going to speak to a group of older, conservative people, but you know they are doing some really great work in the community.

How do I identify with these people where at first glance you might think, "Oh, they don't have anything in common with me."

So (I thought to myself) what is it about this group that I *can* identify with? Like they do charitable work, or they are engaged in their community, or they give back to their community. So the question becomes "What *DO* I have in common with them?" If it's not a common bond, then remember, "I know something they don't and I am bringing that expertise here. They would not have asked me to come and speak if they knew about my subject matter."

This goes back to research and being authentic. I know my subject, I can speak well about my subject— and then leave all that other stuff of, "am I too...?" behind.

Biases exist in both directions: in the listener(s)—what others might think of you, and in you, as speakers—how you might feel different. This feeling of "otherness" or being different can keep us from being truly expressive. Lean into that feeling, address it, and then move on. Embrace what you both believe in and the gift you have to give. This approach transcends our limited thinking—theirs and yours.

Women

One issue that often comes up in coaching sessions and workshops is the difference between how men and women communicate and express themselves. In Western culture, men have been socialized to be direct and assertive in their public speaking, especially when it comes to business. From the boardroom to mainstream media and entertainment, men have been placed or portrayed in more powerful roles.

Women traditionally have not received the same encouragement. While these norms and stereotypes have been shifting, bigger steps are yet to be made, as entertainment attorney, Mishawn Nolan, explains:

> My personal experience has been that women, more than men, are often afraid of living in their power—they are afraid of being powerful.
>
> I think there's certainly some upbringing and societal norms that women are not supposed to be the ones in charge, women are not supposed to be the outspoken

ones because when a woman is really powerful, she's looked at as harsh, pushy, bossy, or a bitch.

And we all [men and women] want to be liked, right? Women want to be liked. And so, they're much more focused sometimes on being liked or being collaborative and part of a team as opposed to really shining and living in their power.

Living in your own power and knowing your worth is a challenge. For some of us, it's more difficult than others, especially when you've not been encouraged or taught how to ask for what you deserve. Tim Curtis has witnessed the male/female difference in the realm of salary negotiation:

A friend who currently has her own business was debating whether to go into the workforce instead. She decided to apply for a corporate job. When she went to the interview, they asked for her salary requirement. She thought, "Well, it should be this amount of money."

She didn't know they actually paid three to four times more for that position. The reality is she's so gifted and wonderful and has enough work experience to demand that higher salary, but didn't believe in herself enough to ask for it.

I think that's probably true much more so of women than men. That's partially why there's a salary gap in most industries—because men are more likely to say, "I'm worth this," versus what women say.

As our societal attitudes shift and change about what it means to be powerful and valuable, activists are leading the cause on how women, in particular, can more fully claim their brilliance and power. Self-esteem expert, speaker, and author, Jess Weiner, is one of them:

> We are both a reflection and a mirror of the culture we consume. So, as women, it's extremely important that we start to tell our own stories. By taking control of the narratives in culture, we begin to eliminate harmful stereotypes and tropes. The stories that get told feature more dynamic and rich characters with juicier plotlines and action. It's those types of characters that both reflect real women in the world and provide new role models for future generations.
>
> It's true that you can't be what you can't see. And in order for more girls to see themselves reflected in the culture they consume, we need more women behind the script, camera, and boardroom table.

What you see in yourself may not be nearly as powerful as what others see in you. But you must believe in the value of what you have to offer so they will value what you have to offer.

We cannot let unfair assessments dim our brilliance, our

unique gifts or our message. How do we change the culture we live in, whether that is pop culture or work culture, where all of us, regardless of sex or any other difference, are truly valued? It starts with how much we value our individual selves.

So ask yourself, "What is it that I deserve?" Assess your worth, then listen to your gut. You are of value. Stand firm to get what you deserve.

CHAPTER 17
Step Up, Speak Out, Be Heard

It starts one voice at a time.

When you decide to speak publicly, it is an act of commitment.

Agreeing to share your thoughts and emotions is a seemingly simple act, but it is what frightens and keeps many of us from speaking at all. When you commit to share your convictions, you also agree to be self-revealing, vulnerable, and open to criticism. To some of us, this is overwhelming. To others, it is exciting.

Either way, what you have to say matters. Your commitment matters. The speaking journey you embark upon with your audience is a choice you make ahead of time.

Before you engage, choose what kind of speaker you are going to be. Will you be nervous and scared, or *fearFULL*? Will you be aligned and fully expressive, or focused on your script?

Once you decide what kind of speaker you're going to be, then the choice can guide you in any situation. Every day you're immersed in some form of public speaking and might not even know it. You engage in public speaking when you're debating a topic with friends, interviewing for a job, teaching a class, giving a keynote, and selling clothes in a retail shop.

You may be called upon to speak unexpectedly, like a eulogy at a funeral, an intervention with a friend or family member, or stand your ground in an argument. In moments like these, you are challenged to balance your raw emotions against what is sensible and appropriate.

One of the most valuable questions for any of these situations is, *"What do I value most right now?"* Is it to speak out, be heard, be right, or reach some common understanding?

When your emotions are elevated, as they might be every time you speak in front of others, it might be best to take a beat. Turn that nervousness into being **fearFULL**. This ensures your message remains focused. Purposeful communication is what public speaking is all about. You honor a commitment to your audience.

I've had the pleasure to study and observe how people communicate and speak publicly in various settings, including the entertainment business, corporate America, and personal development industry in Asia. The collective experiences in working with these different sectors have helped shape this book. With this distinct vantage point in mind, here are a few final thoughts.

Step Up

Own the spotlight. Just like celebrities in the entertainment business, you are a star. Everything you do, from social media to conversations in the office, draws attention to you, one way or another. You are in control of your own public identity. Decide what you want to share with others. It's not a matter of whether or not you are noticed, because you already are. Choose what you want others to see and hear about you. Don't let fear keep you from illuminating your best self.

Speak Out

Know your brand. Just like a business, you have a product, or irresistible offer, that is unique and valuable. Don't sell yourself short or dilute your offer because you're scared that it is not unique or distinct. While others in the audience may share your profession or interests, none of them are exactly you. What you have, others want, but they won't know about it unless you speak. Be purposeful and direct in communicating what it is you have to offer.

Be Heard

Invest in relationships. Building trust is not a one-time task. Your words and actions must be consistent. Also, it is important to advance the conversation. Don't waste time with meaningless words or clichés. Say something meaningful to those who are giving you their time and attention. As a result, you will build respect and reinforce the relationship.

A.W.E.S.O.M.E.

When you own the spotlight, know your brand, and invest in relationships, you are powerful. Your words have meaning. People will listen.

So remember, for purposeful communication embrace your commitment when you speak publicly. Step up. Speak Out. Be Heard. You are A.W.E.S.O.M.E.

SECTION VI:

Reference Guide and Key Terms

A.W.E.S.O.M.E. FLOW CHART

Becoming a better public speaker is an inside-out journey. It doesn't matter if you are nervous or inexperienced; you can learn to present your ideas with ease, precision, and resonance. It starts with an honest look at your fears and what holds you back. Once you address your negative emotions, you can find a sincere connection with your audience that is authentic. Here is a flow chart to help you achieve this goal using the principles discussed in this book.

STEP 01 — Get clear about your offer

- 3 Cs: Clarity, Confidence & Charisma
- CQ: Celebrity Quotient

Result: You understand your innate star quality and its value to others.

STEP 02 — Optimize your personal communication style

- Aligned
- Wired
- Empathetic
- Simple
- Open
- Magical
- Engaging

Result: You create a comprehensive communication experience when you speak.

STEP 03 — Define your desired emotional impact

- Stimulate
- Inspire
- Transform

Result: You establish the direction in which you want to move the audience.

STEP 04 — Create a definitive call to action

- Sell
- Promote
- Entertain
- Activate
- Know

Result: You address your audience with a well-thought-out agenda and put into practice *The A Factor*.

283

15 KEY CONCEPTS FOR BEING A.W.E.S.O.M.E.

The Three Guiding Principles

#1: **You are creative**. You commit your thoughts and ideas out loud into the world and you give birth to something that you no longer hold onto alone.

#2: **You are a subject matter expert**. Your knowledge and conviction of a topic, project, program, or job is based on experiential learning and practice.

#3: **You instinctively know**. Your intuition is usually right. It guides you to the best course of action.

Audience A.I.D.

The roles of individuals with whom you communicate:

Allies. They respect and value what you have to offer. Your communication with them is familiar and less formal. They provide you with a sense of community.

Influencers. They are "in the know" and their stamp of approval is important. Your communication with them is strategic. They legitimize you and your work.

A.W.E.S.O.M.E.

Decision Makers. They are definitive, yes-or-no, people. Your communication with them is deliberate and direct. They determine the results.

A.W.E.S.O.M.E.

Aligned: You are fully expressive; your words, emotions, and intuition are working together in unison to deliver a message and experience.

Wired: You are centered and connected to the context, environment, medium, and purpose of your presentation. You are aware of your place in the overall experience.

Empathetic: You are connected to your audience's feelings, experiences, and values. In turn, they relate to your accomplishments, trials, and passion.

Simple: You get out of your own way. You keep it simple. Your topic and intention guide your talking points, format, technique, and flow.

Open: You embrace the unexpected, stay in the moment, and are connected to the speaking experience.

Magical: You embrace and manifest every communication situation as its own unique experience. No two moments are exactly the same.

Engaging: Your conviction and emotional connection to the subject has value to the audience and draws them to you and your ultimate goal.

Celebrity Essence

Like a celebrity, it is your ability to shine. You show up as your best self, stand tall with your feet planted firmly in the ground, and know with certainty you are a gift to the world.

Celebrity Quotient

CQ is the measure of your *Celebrity Essence*. It starts by identifying three characteristics that authentically and powerfully describe your natural personality. These characteristics are the building blocks of your personal brand.

Communication Disruption

Like static in a phone call or videoconference, it is the moment when your connection to the audience is weak. They may no longer hear you for various different external reasons.

A.W.E.S.O.M.E.

fearFULL

Integrating your fears into your action or speaking. Using fear helps you become a more expressive being. Your audience connects to your authentic expression of emotions.

In Flow

You show up authentically, are fully aligned, immersed into the communication experience, and the right words and actions show up exactly as they need to for that moment.

Irresistible Offer

The undeniable gift you give to others that comes from your true, unique, and authentic being.

Public Speaking

Anytime you purposefully communicate a thought, idea, point of view, or experience to others.

S.I.T.

Three potential impacts you might have on your audience:

15 KEY CONCEPTS FOR BEING A.W.E.S.O.M.E.

Stimulate: You are going to stir up your audience. Get them to think.

Inspire: Lift up their spirits and/or enlighten them in some way.

Transform: Get them to take action.

S.P.E.A.K.

Sell: Your goal is to create a transaction. Your talking points must clearly identify and express how you or your product addresses the needs of your audience. You present the problem and offer solution.

Promote: Your goal is to create awareness and excitement. Your talking points must be descriptive and relevant. You are there to introduce and pitch your audience to something they may not know about and get them emotionally invested.

Entertain: Your goal is to create emotional reaction from your audience. Your stories and anecdotes relate and connect to the lives of your audiences. You provide catharsis, lightness, and/or even encouragement.

Activate: Your goal is to motivate, mobilize or unify your audience toward a personal or common goal. Your points and stories must be passionate, credible, and relevant. You want to awaken others to their own and others' greatest potential.

A.W.E.S.O.M.E.

Know: Your goal is to share knowledge, insight, or wisdom with your audience. Your talking points and stories must be clear, well-organized, and informative. You want to inspire, encourage, and educate others.

Traps

Word Traps: Your focus on words consumes you, so if you miss one in your speech or presentation, you are thrown. You are overly scripted.

Technical Traps: Make sure whatever tool you use enhances what you are going to say. You are not trapped by that technology to make a point. Your message is what matters. Not the bells and whistles.

"Yes" Traps: You focus on what you believe the audience *wants* to hear instead of your message. You already have their time and attention, so give them something valuable—your message or point of view— even if it challenges them.

10 Mantras for Being an A.W.E.S.O.M.E. Speaker

- I am going to show up exactly as I need to in this moment.

- I am aligned. I use my words, emotions, and intuition to fully communicate and express myself.

- I am connected to my higher purpose and wired to my surroundings; I am a gift.

- I open myself up so that my story may stimulate, inspire, and transform others.

- I am the most powerful medium of communication.

- I embrace the unknown and it excites me.

- I am magical: my thoughts, ideas, and words create reality.

- I step into my greatness and empower others to do the same.

- I am A.W.E.S.O.M.E.: **a**ligned, **w**ired, **e**mpathetic, **s**imple, **o**pen, **m**agical, and **e**ngaging.

- I am seen, heard, and powerful. When I speak, people listen.

About the Authors

Jess Ponce III

Recognized as a top media coach and branding expert, Jess Ponce III uses laser-focused training to help professionals from all industries and walks of life strengthen their presentation, leadership, and media skills so they can shine when they need it most—in any speaking arena.

As the author of *Everyday Celebrity: A Personal Branding Guide from a Hollywood Media Coach* and *A.W.E.S.O.M.E: Seven Keys to Unlocking the Speaker Within,* Jess created "The Art of Authentic Self Promotion," also known as "The

A Factor®." His expertise in media communications skills stems from his vast experience in the world of entertainment where he produced and developed programming for ABC, Warner Bros., E! Entertainment, Style, TV Guide Network, and MTV.

He is also the creative force behind Media 2x3, a US-based media company that develops individual branding strategies for influencers, media personalities, and subject matter experts. He also consults and advises TV hosts, Fortune 500 executives, creative professionals, brand ambassadors, and TEDx speakers. Corporate clients include Lucasfilm, The Walt Disney Company, HGTV, LinkedIn, The Ritz Carlton, and BNP Paribas.

Jess co-created multiple communication and public speaking programs for adults and youth as a workshop facilitator and keynote for *The Awesome Group* in Taipei and its affiliates in Hong Kong and Mainland China. In the United States, Jess is a professional speaker based near Hollywood where he helps others find their strengths on leadership presence, brand awareness, crisis communication, and on-camera strategies.

About the Authors

Emily Liu

Emily Liu is founder of AsiaWorks Taiwan, 3rd Hat Consulting, and the Awesome Group. She is a pioneering entrepreneur, business consultant, speaker, and leader in the professional and personal development industry. Her best-in-class, international resources have built multi-media learning platforms in publishing, training programs, premium learning events, and extended product lines.

As a certified corporate and performance coach and Licensed Advanced NLP Practitioner, Emily has more than 20,000 hours of coaching and consulting experiences. Her international client base includes executives from Fortune's Top 500 to entrepreneurs. More than 90,000 people throughout Asia have benefited from programs provided by the Awesome Group.

A.W.E.S.O.M.E.

She co-authored the best-selling *Secrets to Winning* with her mentor Kelly Poulos. Available in four different languages, the principles on performance coaching have been applied by more than 50,000 people worldwide. Corresponding "Secrets to Winning" workshops have also reached mass audiences.

Emily and Hollywood media coach Jess Ponce III co-authored *Everyday Celebrity.* They developed two complimentary workshops, "Superstar Communication" and "Awesome Public Speaking," based on their respective professional experiences in Hollywood and Asia.

Emily lives in Hong Kong, loves to travel, and has the uncanny ability to bring out the best in everyone she meets.

About the Entertainment Professionals Featured in A.W.E.S.O.M.E.

Brian Balthazar is a television host, executive producer and pop culture expert. He is frequently seen as a guest on NBC's *TODAY Show* and *The Wendy Williams Show* to discuss entertainment news and trends. He launched NBC's fourth hour of the *Today Show* with Kathie Lee and Hoda and served as co-executive producer of *The View*. As president of Balthazar Entertainment, he develops programs for television and digital platforms.

Jill Bandemer is a seasoned casting agent who has made her mark on numerous shows for HGTV, Discovery, Bravo, E!, Style Network, Lifetime, WE and more. She cast such notable shows as HGTV's *Bahamas Life*, DIY's *Holmes: Buy It Right*, Lifetime's *Bring It* and the Style Network's *How Do I Look?* She has also booked celebrity interviews for CCTV America, TV Guide Channel, and served as the talent executive for *The Other Half*.

Zachary Bilemdjian is a seasoned costume designer, entertainment costumer, and wardrobe stylist. He has overseen the costume development and production for entertainment offerings at Disneyland and Disney's California Adventure, was part of the costume design launch team for Shanghai Disneyland and Hong Kong Disneyland, and has overseen special projects for Tokyo Disneyland. He's worked on various television programs and specials including Disney Channel's acclaimed *High School Musical 2* and *Jake and the Neverland Pirates*.

Shahnti Olcese Brook is an Emmy and Peabody Award-winning producer who has worked on many variety/entertainment news, talk, and digital media shows for NBC Universal, Paramount, Telepictures, PBS, Syfy, Game Show Network, WarnerMedia, and more. She was instrumental during the creation of the TV Guide Channel, the launch of Reelz Channel, and international expansion of Blackbelt TV. She has cast, produced, and booked thousands of celebrities, influencers, and human-interest stories throughout her career.

Julie Carrier is a trusted authority on leadership development for young women. The CEO of Girls Lead Worldwide, Julie is a #1 national bestselling author, speaker and program consultant. This Emmy nominee has also reached millions on national TV as a confidence coach featured on MTV's positive goal-setting show, *MADE*. She is also a former Senior Management Consultant in Leadership Development for the Pentagon and specializes in neuroscience-based leadership education. Learn more at: www.girlslead.com

Ric Enriquez is a highly respected, Emmy-nominated television producer and casting director. He has worked on highly acclaimed TV shows including *Conan* (TBS), *The Tonight Show* (NBC), *The Pete Holmes Show* (TBS), *Deon Cole's Black Box* (TBS), *Rock of Love* (VH1), *I Love New*

York (VH1), *Jamie Oliver's Dream School* (Sundance), *Celebrity Paranormal Project* (VH1) and *Hollywood Squares* (Sony/KingWorld). His writing and producing credits include: *The Kindness Diaries* (Netflix), *Amazing Adventures of a Nobody: Europe* (Fox Reality).

Jered Gold is a strategic communications and public relations executive focused on creating direct, personal and authentic campaigns that synthesize multifaceted, sometimes complex, information for targeted audiences. He serves as vice president of Marketing and Communications at ArtCenter College of Design, an international leader in art and design education based in Southern California. His industry expertise includes higher education, entertainment, art and design, hospitality, small business, and pop culture enterprise.

Sharon Hashimoto is a creative force with wide ranging talents. Her production credits include being a video editor for *The Insider / Entertainment Tonight*, CBS and Universal, a field director for *Fine Living*, and a writer and editor for Vogue Magazine's quarterly show *TrendWatch*. She has also crafted a talk show pilot for Paramount. Today she continues to develop content, online and off, for a variety of clients ranging from subject matter experts to lifestyle and design brands.

Andi Matheny has over thirty years of experience as an actor, acting coach, TV host and content creator. Andi's television and film credits include *The Resident*, *True Love*

Blooms, *David Makes Man*, and *Lady of the Manor*. Hosting credits include *Essentials*, *Fit Resort & Spa*, *Kwik Witz* and *Friends or Lovers*. She created the award-winning web series *Good Morning St. Pete!* on Amazon Prime. She is the founder of Andi Matheny Acting Studios.

Michael Medico is an actor/director/writer/producer. He's acted on stage, films and in TV shows and has directed acclaimed TV series: *Atypical*, *Grey's Anatomy*, *Good Trouble*, *The Fosters* and *Party of Five*. He created and produced the celebrity-driven *Hot in Hollywood* benefit raising over half a million dollars for international AIDS charities and is on the Western Council of The Actors Fund. He's a graduate of Boston University and lives with his husband and two children in Los Angeles and Campbell River, BC.

Mishawn Nolan is a legal strategist focusing on bespoke solutions for cross-vertical monetization of intellectual property and 360 business optimization. Her clients include companies in lifestyle brands, new media, A/R, V/R and X/R, content creation, children's entertainment, toys, apparel, consumer products, beauty, and technology. Mishawn founded Nolan Heimann LLP in 2013, a woman-owned law firm providing strategic legal advisory services for companies with creative and innovative assets. In addition, Mishawn is an advocate of authentic entrepreneurship.

About the Entertainment Professionals Featured in A.W.E.S.O.M.E.

Amy Prenner is a publicity and marketing dynamo who operates like a producer. At The Prenner Group, she brings her insider knowledge of the business of Hollywood to her clientele. Amy's 20-plus-year career in the entertainment industry has helped her collaborate with some of the biggest and brightest stars in film and television. Personable and approachable, Amy has developed an exclusive network of high-level media contacts, along with an extraordinary eye for strategic communications.

Loren Ruch is Group SVP, Production and Development - HGTV. He oversees the programming team and many of the networks' high profile series and pilots. Prior to HGTV, Loren worked at Fox's *Good Day LA* and *Good Day Live* where he was the recipient of five Emmy awards. He also worked in daytime talk and game shows including *Home & Family, Love Connection* and *Family Feud* and hosts a Facebook Live show called *Mindless Chatter*.

Keylee Sanders is an entrepreneur, blogger, and lifestyle expert. Miss Teen USA in 1995, Keylee moved to Los Angeles to style films, national campaigns, and celebrities. She has been featured in the *Wall Street Journal, Us Weekly, InStyle* magazine, *Yahoo* and other online outlets. She was also an on-camera style expert on E!, Style Network, CBS, ABC, and Fashion TV. She is Vice President of Helmich Luxury Group and the founder of a custom jewelry line featured at www.keyleesanders.com.

A.W.E.S.O.M.E.

Rick Tamlyn is an author, activational keynote speaker, co-active trainer and thought leader. He teaches that every experience, emotion, reaction, and relationship is *All Made Up*. He is a trusted advisor for Fortune 100 companies, small businesses and nonprofits, and has engaged audiences in twenty-two countries. In 2001, Rick co-created *The Bigger Game*, a tool that inspires people to get out of their comfort zones and invent the lives they want. He is the author of *Play Your Bigger Game* (Hay House 2013).

Angelo Tsarouchas You've seen Angelo's face pop up on numerous movie and television shows and his high energy and relatable comedy has made him popular throughout the world. His Amazon Prime Video special *Bigger is Better* has over 14 million viewers and his latest YouTube and Facebook videos have over 10 million views by fans everywhere. www.funnygreek.com

Jess Weiner is CEO of *Talk to Jess*, a consultancy that helps brands better reflect people in their media, marketing, and workplace. Jess's work has created culture-changing moments such as the *Dove Campaign for Real Beauty* and *Barbie's Body Evolution*. She's an acclaimed author, educator, and podcast host of *We're All Going to Die, Anyway*, exploring what it means to live The Good Life, a life you love on your own terms.

Acknowledgments

I am sincerely grateful to all my friends, family, and co-workers for their ongoing support and encouragement.

A special thank you to the wonderful entertainment professionals who generously shared their wisdom with me in this book: *Brian Balthazar, Jill Bandemer, Zachary Bilemdjian, Shahnti Olcese Brook, Julie Carrier, Tim Curtis, Ric Enriquez, Jered Gold, Sharon Hashimoto, Andi Matheny, Michael Medico, Mishawn Nolan, Amy Prenner, Loren Ruch, Keylee Sanders, Rick Tamlyn, Angelo Tsarouchas,* and *Jess Weiner.* Your expertise and insights are invaluable.

To my colleagues who challenge me daily, and my clients, *Nurse Barb Dehn* and *Dr. Deborah Gilboa,* who trust and inspire me, thank you for the opportunities to make a difference. A big shout-out to graphic artists, *Janell Harris, Anne Corneliuson,* and *Paul Guzman,* for adding visual life to my work. To my friend and confidant, *Eleanor Chicolo,* my fabulous editor and mentor, *Sylvia Mendoza,* and my brand manager, *Robin Blakely*—thank you all for keeping the vision and pushing me to be the writer and subject matter expert you know I can be.

To *Emily Liu,* the powerful force who has made all this possible. You are a game changer and I am honored to call you my friend and partner. You and your team, under the wisdom and guidance of *Linda Lu*, have showcased my work in remarkable ways. I will forever be indebted to you.

To my family: knowing you believe in me gives me strength when I need it most. *John*, *Heny* and *Diana Bilemdjian*, thank you for supporting me with kindness and generosity. To my little bro, *Jason Lachenmyer*, I am grateful for your openness, candor, and sense of humor. *Antoinette Ponce*, my dear sister, you mean the world to me... more than you'll ever realize. To my parents, *Jesse Ponce Jr.* and *Patricia Ponce*, thank you for encouraging me to be my best. You were perfect examples. And to my dear *Zachary Bilemdjian*, thank you for being patient, loving, and understanding—and for encouraging me to get out of my own way. I love you and our life together.

And to the awesome *you* out there reading this book, you make it all worth it. Be brilliant and shine.

Testimonials

"As LinkedIn's Head of Infrastructure Engineering, I am frequently asked to speak at events across the globe. This past year I worked with Media 2x3 and Jess Ponce III on transforming my public speaking skill. I received great value out of each of our coaching sessions, whether it was over video conference or in person. Jess's approach and attention to detail was key to my success."

– Zaid Ali,
Senior Director, Infrastructure Engineering, LinkedIn

*

"Working with Jess Ponce has truly been a dream. Jess understands the universality of feelings and has helped me empathize with any audience, whether it's live television and keynote speaking engagements to on-demand webinars and conference presentations. Jess understands that people listen with their entire "being," and so speakers must be able to connect to every aspect of that being. I'm constantly learning from him."

– Nurse Barb Dehn, NP,
On-camera Medical Personality,
www.nursebarb.com

*

A.W.E.S.O.M.E.

"Coaching is a vulnerable space for individuals and teams alike. It takes a special trainer to create a safe space for attendees to learn from the coach, and from each other. Jess masterfully brings everyone along, creating a culture of collaboration and support for each other."

– Adora English,
Senior Manager, Global Communications and
Brand Management, Universal Creative

*

"Jess Ponce knows AWESOME. His guidance, wisdom and coaching have catapulted me to the top of my field. He has made me a far more engaging speaker as I've learned to be more aligned, open and simple in my purpose and delivery. Through his teachings, I've grown my personal brand such that my message is now reaching millions, and my face is recognized on the street!"

– Dr. Deborah Gilboa,
TODAY Show Tastemaker,
Parenting Expert, On-Camera Personality,
www.askdoctorg.com

*

"Jess Ponce dramatically changed my perspective about presentations, storytelling and personal branding. His ability to take an individual with an average message and transform them and their message into a dynamic and engaging presentation is beyond exceptional. His proven

Testimonials

techniques and expertise, coupled with his delightful and fun personality, makes him a top-notch professional.

His techniques and coaching skills were so impactful that we hired him to assist with our entire development team. He was able to work with each person, identifying their strengths and opportunities for increased engagement, connectivity, and impact.

Today, the entire team is AWESOME and excited about their ability to present compelling presentations for the greater good. Jess is amazing! It is truly a privilege and pleasure to work with him and learn from him."

— Laura Pulido,
CCNL Executive Vice President/Chief Financial Officer,
Joni and Friends International Disability Center

*

"Jess Ponce brought an amazing and immediate impact to our event. He juggled executive coaching (remotely!) with a dozen hard-to-pin presenters without missing a step. And he brought it all together in a timeframe I didn't think was possible. Our presenters were twice as good because of Jess!"

— Ben Rogers, Head of Content, Qualtrics

*

A.W.E.S.O.M.E.

"At BNP Paribas Cardif, we invested huge resources to equip our leadership team with the skills of tomorrow. The partnership with Jess, the Hollywood media communication expert, helped our management team build their best authentic executive presence via his professional advice. I look forward to continue working with Jess to build a dream team for our company."

– **See See Ooi**, *Taiwan Country Manager,*
BNP Paribas Cardif

Made in the USA
Coppell, TX
16 November 2022

86486328R00184